The
FRANTIC
FAMILY
COOKBOOK

(Mostly) Healthy Recipes in Minutes

D1302540

by Leanne Ely, C.N.C.

CHAMPION PRESS LTD.

CHAMPION PRESS, LTD.

MILWAUKEE, WISCONSIN

ISBN 1-189400-11-8 ~ LCCN 2002103112

Manufactured in the USA 20 19 18 17 16 15 14 13 12 11 10 9 8

Dedication

This book is dedicated to my mother, Miriam. A great cook, wonderful mom and all-around, great gal.

Acknowledgments

A thousand thanks to the many taste testers (some of whom are named, others that are not) for helping to shape these recipes into what they are today. To David Lawrence Dewey, whose wisdom and mentoring have helped me follow a clearer path. To Mindy Henderson and Brook Noel for the QVC opportunities—thank you for believing in me.

A special thanks...

Leanne Ely and Champion Press would like to send a special thank you to the wonderful families that taste-tested the many recipes throughout this book. You'll find their quotes and comments throughout the book.

THE MEWOLLER FAMILY
CANDACE MAHONEY
KIM SCHULTZ
LESLIE CLARK
SHARON JOHNSTON
MARIE SMYTHE
SANDYE DELPH
MICHELLE MCLAUGHLIN
MEGAN WOLFE
JEANNETTE TULIS
EILEEN MEWOLLER
WENDI KITZMAN
BRENDA RODE
DONNA SMITH
CARA WEIFESHOFF
JILL CAFFERTY
IVY WEINER

Also By Leanne Ely:

Healthy Foods: an irreverent guide to understanding nutrition and feeding your family well

A Healthy Unit for Practical Nutrition and Wellness – Grades K-5

A Healthy Unit for Practical Nutrition and Wellness – Grades 6-9

The Curriculum Yellow Pages (co-author)

CONTENTS

★ Foreword

Looking for ways to save some time or a buck has almost become a national pastime. For a lot of people, looking for less expensive ways to live stems from necessity; for others it's hip to be tight. Being conservative with your cash or your time makes a person necessarily creative—especially in the kitchen. Even if money isn't tight and you're just trying to get the most bang for your buck, there are ways of doing things less expensively without sacrificing style and taste. And one of the most effective ways to see that played out is with your grocery dollar.

I am one who believes that living on a tight budget (both cash-wise and time-wise) needn't be an exercise in a meager, Spartan existence. Preparation, spices, ethnic cuisine all come into play in the kitchen, making even "mere beans" into something spectacular. That is the goal of this book--making cheap eats into food fit for a king and doing it fast.

Keeping servings under .99 cents wasn't too tough. However, after having a few recipes tested, I found prices varied greatly from tester to tester. Sometimes the prices per serving varied considerably and the reason was either the difference in price from region to region in different parts of the country or, more importantly, that the particular tester happened to get chicken (or whatever else) on sale that week at the grocery store. That same principle plays itself out even more dramatically when you throw a salvage or grocery outlet into the equation and you get the food at a deep discount. The pricing in this book is just a starting place—you may even do better in some cases because of what you have available to you in the way of discount stores, outlets, and of course, time. For some people, the pricing could be too low because of those same factors. Like automobile manufacturers always say, "your mileage may vary."

Nothing in this book would be considered gourmet, foodie food; just honest-to-goodness, delicious, inexpensive family food—with most of it being pretty healthy. There's an occasional heftier-than-usual meal, but you can live with that, right? As best we can, we give our families healthy food. We make tasty meals and sometimes they are a little heavier than what is optimal. Balance is the secret to being able to pull that off every once in a while. Having a heavier than usual meal once a week won't kill you—just keep it in perspective and keep in mind that Double Cheeseburger Casserole has your name on it!

✫ INTRODUCTION
How to feed a Frantic Family
(and do it inexpensively)

The days of making multi-coursed meals and spending hours getting dinner on the table have gone the way of June Cleaver's girdle. You are as likely to see a woman spending two hours preparing dinner as you are to seeing her vacuum in high heels and pearls—it ain't gonna happen!

We have become frantic families by the mere pace in which we live. I could pontificate ad nauseum about the value of not being so busy, but will it make a difference? Children still have sports, music lessons and after-school activities. Mom most likely has a job. The world has changed. Today's families need quick, nutritious meals—it's a fact and it's a critical one at that. No one wants dinner at 7:30 every night. And while the crock-pot is one of the most wonderful tools a kitchen can have, you don't want crockpot meals every night either. This cookbook, like my first book, *Healthy Foods*, is full of good food families love, with recipes you will actually use—not just peruse! The recipes are practical, healthy, and have all been taste tested by real life families all over America. If they didn't pass muster, they didn't make it into this book.

So…how does one feed a frantic family and do it inexpensively? It's starts with a very simple premise: you start with inexpensive ingredients. You just have to have a few basics down before you even attempt to cook…especially if your goal is cooking as inexpensively as possible. Convenience foods are (for the most part) banished because of expense and the fact that they're usually more chemicals than food. But don't fret! It's not difficult cooking "from scratch" (though I really loathe that term—sounds like slaving over a hot stove all day!).

The first thing to consider before even leaving the house to go grocery shopping isn't your list, but what you already have in your pantry. A well-stocked pantry is the first component in being able to get a frantic family fed. The more time you spend running to the store for a couple of onions or a can of tomatoes, the more time you have wasted. Having a pantry filled with stuff you use is critical. (Plus, you won't be tempted to impulse spend and blow your budget).

After giving your pantry the once over, you can make your list and check it twice. If you want to really maximize your grocery dollar, I've found some great angles that will help accomplish this goal. For starters, you can do some sleuthing to find the best deals. Some of the easiest to find, and most effective, bargains are found in those annoying grocery store flyers stuck in the middle of your local newspaper. The big sales on the front of these flyers are called "loss leaders" and that's what they use to lure you in, but their evil and wicked scheme is to tempt you to buy everything—even the overpriced stuff—right there.

Resist the siren's call! And beware of other traps too, like the end caps at the tops and the bottoms of the aisles. It's a psychological thing; all those cans stacked to the ceiling must surely be on sale. But it ain't necessarily so. Make sure you check the signage before you load your cart.

A lot of people find using double coupons and scoring a good deal to be a cheap thrill. I totally understand that—I've bought toothpaste for a penny before—you can't help but feel smug! Coupons can be handy and can possibly save you some serious cash, but be aware that a lot of the foods promoted through coupons are overly processed and usually overly priced as well. Most of them probably won't be used in this book. Decide if the time invested in clipping coupons is really worth it. I always check the coupons, rarely clip them and when I do, forget to use them. But there are always exceptions to this rule and sometimes it's worth the running around to score an amazing deal on something. For the most part, finding two or three markets that have good loss leaders is enough. You don't want to spend your life ever on the prowl for the next red hot grocery deal, but it really is worth going to a couple of different markets to be able to take advantage of loss leaders.

When you consider that the average family of four spends well over $100 weekly in groceries, it's well worth the extra effort to be slightly inconvenienced. I spend less than half of that for my household and we eat very well and a good many of the recipes in this book are what we eat!

To get the rest of your groceries, you may want to consider an outlet or off-brand type of grocery store and steer clear of regular grocery stores unless trying to hunt down loss leaders. Some people prefer the convenience of one-stop shopping, but you need to remember you always end up paying for that convenience. You need to weigh and measure for yourself what your bottom line is and then be willing to pay one way or the other—either a small investment in time or a small investment in your pocketbook.

You might want to try a local outlet or salvage place next time you shop, just to see if this way of shopping works for you. To find one in your area, ask some penny-pinching friends where they shop. Look in the yellow pages under "salvage" or "surplus" and see what you find. You'll be amazed—a lot of times, one of these little money saving treasure troves has been sitting there under your nose for years.

Another place for cheap-o ingredients is the back of the regular grocery store for the dent and bent stuff. I bought a dozen big boxes of Grape-Nuts there for $1.00/box awhile back. Some were expired and some were dented. The cereal was fine and I saved a fortune. My general rule of thumb for buying cold cereal is that it has to be less than .10/ounce, but that is only in the case of true desperation. 95% of the time, I buy my cereal for $1.00 a box. Do the math and you'll never pay retail again.

But what about those humongous warehouse stores? A lot of people are convinced that $35.00 per year memberships to these clubs are proof positive that they are being thrifty. Let me assure you that is often not the case and, in fact, you may even be getting gouged. If you don't know your prices walking into one of these places—you might end up getting shnookered—or run over by an over zealous teenager on a forklift. Just because you buy the megaton-sized spaghetti sauce, doesn't mean you have bought inexpensively. It used to be that the bigger the container, the cheaper the product. Retailers have begun purposely raising prices on larger sizes because the public believes this. Sneaky, huh? Make sure you check the price per ounce before buying large.

Another problem with these big clubs is the temptation to overbuy because it's a deal or to buy stuff that isn't on your list. No matter how cost-effective it may seem, if you've overspent or bought stuff not on your list, your budget will be out of whack.

Cutting food costs through smart shopping is one of the easiest ways to get a handle on your budget. A few smart tactics and it can be done—tastefully, healthfully and with style.

Chapter 1:
Soup-Less Casseroles
or Yes, you can make a good casserole without ever opening a can of soup

In the past 40 years, canned cream-of-whatever soup has taken on another life form in the cooking arena. There are cookbooks dedicated to this pursuit and a large following of people who pride themselves on what they can do with a can of cream of tomato. But have you ever opened one of those cans and really looked at it, in all its gelatinous glory? I am to the point in my life where I have simply seen one too many casserole recipes made with some kind of *Cream of What's-It* soup. It is more than possible to make fabulous casseroles without a can of soup being the main ingredient. In fact, it's easy and relatively painless.

If you're finding this concept difficult and are in denial, follow this simple exercise. Go over to the cupboard, open the door and give your regrets to the Cream of Mushroom. Repeat after me, "Farewell, dear soup. It was nice knowing you." Good byes are important—you need to get on with your cooking. No use crying over 800 milligrams of sodium lost in a can of soup.

Casseroles are wonderful creatures— they are fast and easy to make, freeze great, and are a snap to reheat—the perfect comfort food to serve for just about any occasion, company included. They are the one-stop dinner—from baking dish to dinner plate, it's just that simple. How can you not love that? Throw a little salad or a steamed vegetable into the mix and bada bing, bada bang—dinner.

So without further ado, bring on the casserole recipes!

Cheap-o Cassoulet
Serves 4

Repeat after me, class—CASS oh LAY (it's French, but not fancy!) The French have made this one for years, and secrets and mysteries abound on how it is made. There is usually duck in it, (that takes a few days to prepare) sausages, lamb, chicken—a hugely arduous process for mere mortals. This recipe takes the best of what cassoulet has to offer and simplifies it for the rest of the world. The result is truly delicious. I know you'll love it as much as the taste testers!

½ pound lean beef, cut up
  olive oil spray
4 carrots, thinly sliced
4 leeks, thinly sliced
2 small onions, chopped
4 slices turkey bacon, chopped
  (optional ingredient)
4 cloves garlic, pressed
1⅓ cups navy beans (one can),
  drained (or use your own
  cooked beans)

1 cup red wine (dry)
½ teaspoon thyme
salt and pepper to taste
2 bay leaves
2 (14 oz.) cans tomatoes,
  un-drained
½ cup dried bread crumbs
  (make yourself from heels of
  bread – toast and crush)
2 cloves garlic, pressed
1 tablespoon parsley (you can
  use dried or double for
  fresh)

Preheat oven to 350 degrees. Trim fat from beef and cut into ¾ inch cubes. Set aside. Coat a large nonstick skillet with olive oil cooking spray (see sidebar on cooking spray) and place over medium heat until hot. Add carrots and next 4 ingredients; cover and cook for about 5 minutes. Add beef and cook for another 3 minutes or until browned, stirring occasionally. Add beans and next 5 ingredients; stir well. Bring to a boil over medium-high heat, and cook, uncovered for about 5 minutes, stirring as needed. Discard the bay leaves. Combine bread crumbs, parsley, and garlic, and set aside. Plop your cassoulet mixture into a 2 or 3 quart baking dish. Spread bread crumb mixture over the top and bake for 25 minutes or until bread crumbs are browned.

PER SERVING: 472 CALORIES (KCAL); 13G TOTAL FAT; (25% CALORIES FROM FAT); 25G PROTEIN; 57G CARBOHYDRATE; 47MG CHOLESTEROL; 809MG SODIUM. FOOD EXCHANGES: 2 GRAIN (STARCH); 2 LEAN MEAT; 5 ½ VEGETABLE; 0 FRUIT; 1 FAT; 0 OTHER CARBOHYDRATES

What's with the oil spray?

I am anti-aerosol when it comes to oil sprays. Without naming names, my opinion of these commercial sprays isn't positive. They are full of propellant and that is fine if you're an airplane. But you're not. Neither are your children, so stick with real food that is worthy of consumption. There are oil sprayers available everywhere now. I saw one in Wal-Mart just recently and I know the Pampered Chef™ people put out a popular one. Another brand is called Misto™ and they even have a website (www.misto.com). I consider this little contraption an excellent investment.

To use, fill the sprayer with a good oil (like olive oil) and keep in a dark cupboard or refrigerator so it won't get rancid (-keeping something like this on the stove isn't a very good idea). I have two and keep one filled with olive oil in my cupboard and another with regular safflower oil in the fridge.

CASSOULET COMMENTS

"This is tasty, even my fussy son who generally doesn't like casseroles, told me twice with his mouth full, 'this is good!'"

Pork Chop Casserole with Apples

Serves 4

This is a wonderful dish in the fall when apples are at their peak. It wouldn't be a big deal to substitute chicken when making this dish— as a matter of fact, one of our testers did and she loved it!

4 pork chops (whatever you can get on sale—not too thick, but not wafer thin, either)
1 tablespoon olive oil
2 large potatoes, sliced
1 medium onion, sliced

salt and pepper to taste
¼ teaspoon nutmeg
2 apples – cored, peeled and cut into wedges
1¼ cup apple juice
1 tablespoon cornstarch

In a large skillet, brown chops on both sides in olive oil on medium high heat. Remove from skillet and arrange in a 2-quart casserole. Add potato slices and onion to skillet. Heat thoroughly, stirring carefully to get up all the bits from the bottom of the pan. Sprinkle with salt, a little pepper and nutmeg. Stir in apple wedges. Spoon mixture over chops. Add 1 cup apple juice to the skillet and heat until just starting to simmer. Pour over apple-potato mixture. Cover casserole and bake in a 350 degree oven for 45 minutes or until chops and vegetables are tender. Using a slotted spoon, place apple-potato mixture on plate and arrange chops on top. Combine remaining ¼ cup apple juice and cornstarch; stir until lump-free. Pour into pan juices, cook until thickened, stirring constantly. Serve sauce over chops or separately, as desired.

PER SERVING: 405 CALORIES (KCAL); 19G TOTAL FAT; (41% CALORIES FROM FAT); 25G PROTEIN; 35G CARBOHYDRATE; 74MG CHOLESTEROL; 65MG SODIUM. FOOD EXCHANGES: 1 GRAIN (STARCH); 3½ LEAN MEAT; ½ VEGETABLE; 1 FRUIT; 1½ FAT; 0 OTHER CARBOHYDRATES

TASTE TESTER COMMENTS:

"This was the biggest surprise! I really didn't see anyone in my family liking apples in this recipe but I had an assignment to complete. I was SO wrong! We have 5 people in our family and they were dipping the pork chop bones in the sauce and sucking it off the bone. I know this sounds gross but it is the sign of a GREAT meal."

Easy Fiesta Casserole

Serves 6

In my last book, *Healthy Foods: An Irreverent Guide to Understanding Nutrition,* I gave you the recipe for my hit casserole, Enchilasagna. This recipe isn't a clone, but a distant cousin with a crunchy texture and a slightly different flavor for a change of pace. As I advised with Enchilasagna, you can turn Easy Fiesta Casserole into something completely different by substituting chicken for the beef. If doing so you would use 2 cups cooked and chopped chicken meat.

1 pound ground beef
1 (15 oz.) can pinto beans
1 cup jarred salsa (your
    choice on temperature!)
2 tablespoons taco sauce
2 teaspoons cumin (I use way
    more, like about 4 teaspoons)

1 teaspoon garlic powder
2 cups coarsely broken tortilla
    chips (I use baked chips)
1 cup sour cream (I use low-fat)
2 green onions, sliced
1 medium tomato, chopped
1 cup shredded cheese (jack or
    cheddar, your choice)
Shredded lettuce and taco sauce
    or whatever else you like.

Heat oven to 350 degrees. Cook beef in a skillet over a medium-high heat till browned and drain well. Stir in beans, salsa, 2 tablespoons taco sauce, cumin and garlic powder. Heat to boiling, stirring occasionally. Place tortilla chips in an un-greased 2-quart casserole dish. Then, top with beef mixture, then spread some sour cream and sprinkle a little bit of the onions, tomato and cheese. Bake uncovered for about 25 minutes or until hot and bubbly. Arrange additional tortilla chips around edge of casserole for a more "feast-ive" look. Serve with lettuce and taco sauce or whatever else you deem appropriate for Taco Casserole Night. We like chopped stuff: cilantro, lettuce, onion, tomato, plus sour cream and lots more salsa.

PER SERVING: 660 CALORIES (KCAL); 18G TOTAL FAT; (24% CALORIES FROM FAT); 36G PROTEIN; 88G CARBOHYDRATE; 59MG CHOLESTEROL; 819MG SODIUM FOOD EXCHANGES: 5½ GRAIN (STARCH); 3 LEAN MEAT; ½ VEGETABLE; 0 FRUIT; 2 FAT; 0 OTHER CARBOHYDRATES

Chicken, Broccoli, and Brown Rice Casserole

Serves 8

This rich casserole is an easy translation of typical, add-a-can-o' soup casseroles. It has the same creamy effect as the soup-laden version, only much healthier and, to be honest, I think the flavor is better! For the record, I add a lot more seasoning, but keep it tame for less bold palates—it's much easier to add a little more later.

5 cups cooked brown rice
salt and pepper to taste
1 teaspoon oregano
2 teaspoons garlic powder
salt and pepper to taste
4½ cups coarsely chopped
    fresh broccoli florets
    (or use frozen)
1 (32 oz.) container of sour
    cream (low-fat)

1 egg white
¾ cup Romano cheese, divided
1 teaspoon basil
1½ teaspoons paprika
2 eggs
¼ cup flour
3 green onions, thinly sliced
2 cups cooked chicken, chopped

Combine first 5 ingredients in a bowl; stir well, and set aside. Drop broccoli into a large saucepan of boiling water; cook 3 minutes (only if fresh). Drain and set aside. Combine flour, eggs, and egg white in a large bowl and stir well with a wire whisk. Add ½ cup plus 2 tablespoons Romano cheese and the next 5 ingredients; stir well, and set aside. Spoon half of the rice mixture into a lightly greased 13 x 9 inch baking dish. Arrange the chicken over rice mixture and top with green onions. Spread half of the sour cream mixture evenly over green onions. Then spoon the remaining rice mixture over sour cream mixture. Arrange broccoli over rice, and spread the remaining sour cream mixture evenly over broccoli. Combine remaining 2 tablespoons Romano cheese and ½ teaspoon of paprika; sprinkle over casserole. Bake in a preheated 350 degree oven for 30 minutes, or until golden and bubbly.

PER SERVING: 322 CALORIES (KCAL); 9G TOTAL FAT; (23% CALORIES FROM FAT); 22G PROTEIN; 40G CARBOHYDRATE; 96MG CHOLESTEROL; 208MG SODIUM. FOOD EXCHANGES: 2 GRAIN (STARCH); 2 ½ LEAN MEAT; ½ VEGETABLE; 0 FRUIT; ½ FAT; 0 OTHER CARBOHYDRATES

Very Nice Chicken & Rice Casserole

Serves 4

This very delicious and easy to prepare recipe takes just a few minutes to put together and is a major league hit in our household. It would be simple to change the seasoning and completely change the flavor of the casserole. Try substituting curry powder for Italian seasoning and see what you think!

1½ cups chicken broth
1 cup brown rice (not cooked)
1 small onion, chopped
½ cup mozzarella cheese
1½ teaspoons Italian seasoning
2 teaspoons garlic powder
salt and pepper to taste
¼ cup Romano cheese

1 (15 oz.) can whole tomatoes-rained and chopped
4 boneless, skinless chicken breasts (or use something cheaper if you like-you may have to extend cooking time though)
½ teaspoon garlic powder
1½ teaspoons Italian seasoning
salt and pepper

Combine first 9 ingredients in a lightly greased 2-quart casserole and stir well. Arrange chicken breast halves over rice mixture, and sprinkle with garlic powder and a little salt and pepper. Sprinkle with Romano cheese and 1½ teaspoons Italian seasoning. Cover and bake at 375 degrees for 45 minutes. Uncover and bake an additional 15 minutes or until liquid is absorbed.

PER SERVING: 557 CALORIES (KCAL); 11G TOTAL FAT; (17% CALORIES FROM FAT); 67G PROTEIN; 46G CARBOHYDRATE; 157MG CHOLESTEROL; 595MG SODIUM. FOOD EXCHANGES: 2½ GRAIN (STARCH); 8½ LEAN MEAT; 1½ VEGETABLE; 0 FRUIT; 1 FAT; 0 CARBOHYDRATES

TASTE TESTER COMMENTS:

"We loved this one! A real hit. We had a buy-one-get-one-free sale on chicken breasts at our local grocery store, so the cost wasn't too much."

Chicken & 'Chokes Casserole

Serves 12

This casserole requires a little more work than some of the others, but it's worth the effort, plus you can freeze the leftovers for another great meal; or reheat them for a second easy meal or great lunch.

2 tablespoons olive oil	1 tablespoon thyme
12 chicken thighs, skinned	2½ cup frozen peas, (petite
4 cloves of garlic, pressed	peas are best)
3 onions, chopped	1 (15 oz.) can diced tomatoes
2 cups brown rice (not cooked)	1 tablespoon thyme
3 cups chicken broth	1 cup white wine
½ tablespoon sage	
1 jar marinated artichoke hearts,	
chopped	

Heat a tablespoon of olive oil in a 5 quart Dutch oven over medium heat. Add chicken and lightly salt and pepper, then cook 7 minutes on each side or until lightly browned. Add a little water if the chicken starts to stick. Pull mixture from pot and set aside. Add another tablespoon of oil to your Dutch oven and add onion, garlic and rice. Sauté 15 minutes or until rice is lightly browned. Add broth and next 5 ingredients and bring to a boil. Then add your chicken mixture to the pot and top with tomatoes and artichokes. Bake uncovered at 400 degrees for 45 minutes or so, remembering to stir mid-point. Add frozen peas, cover casserole and cook 5-10 minutes or until liquid is absorbed.

PER SERVING: 285 CALORIES (KCAL); 7G TOTAL FAT; (21% CALORIES FROM FAT); 20G PROTEIN; 33G CARBOHYDRATE; 57MG CHOLESTEROL; 298MG SODIUM. FOOD EXCHANGES: 2 GRAIN(STARCH); 2 LEAN MEAT; 1 VEGETABLE; 0 FRUIT; ½ FAT; 0 OTHER CARBOHYDRATES

TASTE TESTER COMMENTS:

"YUM! My kids went ape over this one! This was delicious! I would serve this to my mother-in-law (wow!). When I fix it again, I'm going to cook the garlic with the onions and rice because it burned a little when I put it with the chicken. The recipe serves 12 but each of my kids ate 2 pieces of chicken so it really only served 6 people in my family."
Cost per serving: $ 0.60

Tiny's Two Ton Weekend Lasagna

Serves 12

Here's a recipe not known for its lightness and inability to add dimension to your thighs. And it takes more time than usual to make—notice the word "weekend" in the title. The good part is that you'll love eating this; the bad part is the portion size. See how small I made them? Unless you want to count fat cells, my suggestion is you go easy and make plenty of steamed vegetables and a hearty salad. Food like this shouldn't be forbidden—just kicked down a notch or two!

For the sauce use:
1 stick butter
½ cup flour
4 cups milk

For chicken filling use:
1 teaspoon oregano
½ teaspoon thyme
1 small box frozen spinach, thawed, drained and chopped
1½ cups mushrooms, sliced
5 cups cooked chicken, chopped

2 tablespoons butter
2 cloves garlic
2 tablespoons dry white wine
1 (15 oz.) container of ricotta cheese (I use low-fat)
1 large egg
15 sheets of no-cook lasagna noodles
½ cup Romano cheese, grated
shot of Tabasco

Preheat oven to 350 degrees and lightly grease a 13 x 9-inch baking dish. In a saucepan melt butter over medium-low heat. Whisk in flour, making a roux (a thick paste), stirring constantly for about 2 minutes. Add milk slowly and bring mixture to a gentle boil, whisking until thick and smooth. Add salt and pepper to taste and simmer sauce over low heat, whisking occasionally until thickened—about 10 minutes or so. Transfer sauce to a bowl and cover surface with a piece of plastic wrap after it's cooled a bit (to avoid a skin on your sauce). Next, in a small bowl crumble oregano and thyme. In a large skillet melt butter over moderate heat and cook chicken, garlic, and half the herbs, stirring occasionally for 5 minutes, or until chicken is cooked through. Transfer chicken with a slotted spoon to a large bowl. Add wine to your skillet and bring mixture to a boil, all the while stirring. Add mushrooms and spinach and cook, covered, until spinach is wilted. Add remaining garlic, herbs, a conservative shot of Tabasco, salting and peppering to taste. Cook, stirring occasionally, until mushrooms are no longer swimming in their own liquid. Add mushroom mixture to chicken and stir until combined well. Reserving 1 cup sauce, add remaining sauce to chicken mixture and stir until combined well. In a bowl whisk together ricotta, egg, basil, and salt and pepper to taste. Pour ½ cup reserved sauce into baking dish. Although the sauce won't cover the entire baking dish, try to evenly distribute it on the bottom. Cover with 3 sheets of pasta, making sure they do not touch each other. Spread half of chicken mixture over pasta sheets and top with another 3 pasta sheets. Spread half of ricotta mixture over pasta and top with another 3 pasta sheets. Continue to layer until you end with sauce over the top and a sprinkling of Romano cheese.

PER SERVING: 836 CALORIES (KCAL); 27G TOTAL FAT; (30% CALORIES FROM FAT); 52G PROTEIN; 92G CARBOHYDRATE; 461MG CHOLESTEROL; 396MG SODIUM. FOOD EXCHANGES: 5½ GRAIN(STARCH); 5 LEAN MEAT; ½ VEGETABLE; 0 FRUIT; 3 FAT; 0 OTHER CARBOHYDRATES

TASTE TESTER COMMENTS:

"YIKES! This was too good! Don't tell me about the fat grams in it and ruin it. It was wonderful."
Cost per serving: .88

Baked Ziti Con Queso

Serves 8

Can it get better than this? This casserole dish is simply fabulous—the flavor and cheeses make an incredible combination. Don't miss out on this dish. Serve with a rustic salad and some garlic bread to push everything around on your plate.

2 tablespoons olive oil
1 onion, chopped
3 large garlic cloves, pressed
⅓ cup tomato paste
1 8-ounce can tomato sauce
1 cup water
1 teaspoon oregano, crumbled
½ teaspoon sage
½ cup grated Romano cheese

1 (15 oz.) container ricotta cheese
1 egg
8 ounces mozzarella cheese, grated
1 pound cooked ziti or other tubular pasta

Preheat oven to 425 degrees. Lightly grease a 9 X 13 baking dish. Heat oil in heavy, large saucepan over medium-low heat. Add onion and garlic and cook until onion is soft about 3 minutes. Mix in tomato paste and cook another minute. Add tomato sauce, water, oregano and sage. Simmer until mixture thickens slightly, stirring occasionally, about 10 minutes. Stir in ¼ cup Romano cheese. Salt and pepper to taste. In medium bowl combine ricotta cheese and egg. Reserve ¼ cup mozzarella cheese for topping. Add remaining mozzarella to ricotta cheese mixture and blend. Season with salt and pepper. Now put this thing together like a lasagna. Start with the tomato sauce on the bottom of the baking dish. Next, layer 1/3 of pasta over. Drop half of ricotta cheese mixture over by the spoonful. Then put the sauce on next and continue layering until it's done. Top with remaining mozzarella cheese and bake for 30 to 40 minutes.

PER SERVING: 432 CALORIES (KCAL); 15G TOTAL FAT; (32% CALORIES FROM FAT); 24G PROTEIN; 49G CARBOHYDRATE; 39MG CHOLESTEROL; 391MG SODIUM

TASTE TESTER COMMENTS:

"Huge hit at my house. Everyone wanted seconds. I had everything in my pantry already (that was a bonus) but I figure it was still very inexpensive to prepare, around 65 cents a serving."

Aunt Martha's Fabulous Chicken Spaghetti Casserole

Serves 10

4 cups chicken, cooked and diced
1 pound spaghetti, cooked (al dente—not overcooked)
3 tablespoons butter, divided
2 tablespoons flour
½ cup milk
1 (15 oz.) can chicken broth
1 cup mayonnaise (I use low-fat)
1 cup sour cream (I use low-fat)
1 cup Romano cheese
⅓ cup white wine
1 teaspoon garlic powder
1 teaspoon Dijon mustard
salt and pepper to taste
8 ounces fresh mushrooms, sliced

Make a basic white sauce by melting 2 tablespoons butter in a pan, whisking in the flour and cooking until bubbly. Add milk and chicken broth, stirring and cooking until thickened. Set aside and cool slightly; then add mayonnaise, sour cream, cheese, wine, mustard, salt and pepper, stirring well to incorporate. Sauté mushrooms in remaining butter. Place mushrooms, chicken, and spaghetti in a 3 quart casserole dish. Add sauce and mix well. Sprinkle additional Romano cheese on the top. Bake at 350 degrees for 30 minutes.

PER SERVING: 402 CALORIES (KCAL); 12G TOTAL FAT; (27% CALORIES FROM FAT); 30G PROTEIN; 41G CARBOHYDRATE; 82MG CHOLESTEROL; 491MG SODIUM. FOOD EXCHANGES: 2½ GRAIN(STARCH); 3 LEAN MEAT; 0 VEGETABLE; 0 FRUIT; 1½ FAT; 0 OTHER CARBOHYDRATES

TASTE TESTER COMMENTS:

"Another keeper, although I did have to fish mushrooms out of the kids' portions—more for me! Keep them coming—my kids think I've suddenly become Super Chef!"
Cost per serving: .89

Chickles and Dunkles Casserole

Serves 6

My friend Jann used to call her Chicken and Dumplings, Chickles and Dunkles—I thought it was a fun name, so I snagged it. (hope you don't mind, Jann!) This recipe is mine though...not Jann's. Enjoy!

½ cup milk
1 tablespoon oil
1 cup flour
1 teaspoon baking powder
6 boneless chicken breasts (no skin or with skin is fine)
1 medium onion, finely chopped
1 stalk celery, finely chopped
2 carrots, sliced
1 teaspoon thyme
salt and pepper to taste
2 (15 oz) cans chicken broth

Preheat oven to 325 degrees. Lightly grease a 3 quart casserole dish. In a medium bowl, combine milk and oil. Gradually stir in flour, baking powder, and ¼ teaspoon salt. Mix well into a dough consistency and set aside. Place raw chicken breasts in the bottom of the casserole dish. Cover chicken with onions, celery and carrots. Evenly sprinkle the thyme, salt and pepper over the vegetables. Pour broth over everything. With your hands, form 2-inch balls from the dough and drop them on top of the casserole. Cover tightly and bake for 1 hour. Remove cover and bake for an additional 10 minutes or so, if you like your dumplings slightly browned (like I do), or leave covered and cook an additional 15 minutes.

PER SERVING: 410 CALORIES (KCAL); 7G TOTAL FAT; (15% CALORIES FROM FAT); 61G PROTEIN; 22G CARBOHYDRATE; 140MG CHOLESTEROL; 711MG SODIUM. FOOD EXCHANGES: 1 GRAIN(STARCH); 8 LEAN MEAT; 1 VEGETABLE; 0 FRUIT; ½ FAT; 0 OTHER CARBOHYDRATES

Chapter 2
GRIND IT, BABY:
GROUND BEEF MAGIC

Ground beef is one of those ingredients that is a must-have in any frantic family's fridge or freezer. Even if you don't eat beef, there is something ground up that will work just as well, be it chicken, turkey, pork or even TVP (texturized vegetable protein).

Another very cool thing about ground beef is being able to do most of the cooking in one skillet. Packaged skillet-style dinners have become quite popular in recent years because of their ability to minimize clean-up. You can make something even more tasty without a boxed mix and save your family money. Not to mention, you won't bombard them with chemical additives, colorings and flavor enhancers. Who needs that?

Ground beef is a virtual smorgasbord waiting to happen. One little package of ground beef can mean so many different things for dinner—meatloaf, chili, hamburgers, pasta sauces, hash—lots of fun options and almost all of them, fast and easy, too.

TEN FAST AND EASY THINGS TO DO WITH A PACKAGE OF GROUND BEEF

- **Make hamburgers!** Shape one pound of meat into four ½" thick patties. Cook as usual and serve with all your favorite fixin's.
- **Mexi-beef on rice:** Brown beef, drain fat and add taco seasoning. Serve on top of brown rice with a little cheese, salsa and a tortilla for pushing.
- **Quick Nachos:** Brown beef, drain fat and add taco seasoning. Serve on top of tortilla chips, add salsa and shredded cheese. Bake for 5 minutes in a 400 degree oven, or until cheese is melted. Serve with additional salsa and sour cream.
- **A Peek of Greek:** Brown beef, drain fat and add Greek seasoning. Serve with pita bread, cucumbers, tomatoes, onions and plain yogurt.
- **No-Brainer Spaghetti:** Brown beef, drain fat and season with Italian seasoning, garlic powder, salt and pepper. Add favorite canned or jarred spaghetti sauce.
- **Easier than Easy Lasagna:** Do the same as above, but layer uncooked noodles, swiped with ricotta in a 9 x 11 pan, alternating with meat sauce, noodles with ricotta, mozzarella, sauce, etc., till done. Don't top with cheese. Cover with tented foil and bake 1 hour on 375 degrees. When finished, top with mozzarella cheese and continue baking for 5 minutes more, till cheese is melted.
- **Curried beef on rice:** Brown beef, drain fat and season with curry powder, garlic, salt and pepper to taste, add 1 small can (6 oz.) tomato sauce, correct seasoning and serve on prepared rice.
- **Quick Hamburger Soup:** I have a similar recipe in my first book, *Healthy Foods.* This one is even easier: brown beef, drain fat and season with garlic powder, thyme, salt and pepper to taste. Add ½ cup chopped onion, 1 can chopped tomatoes with juice, 1 can chicken broth and 1 cup frozen veggie medley. Top with a little cheese when finished cooking.
- **Frisco Burgers:** Make long, skinny burgers and serve on grilled sourdough with cheese and sautéed onions, along with Thousand Island dressing for dipping.
- **Sloppy Joes:** Brown beef, drain fat, and season with garlic powder, salt and pepper. Add ½ an onion and cook a little more, then add ½ cup barbecue sauce, 16oz. can tomato sauce and simmer for 5 minutes. Serve on top of hamburger buns. Variation: to make it a Sloppy José, add ¾ cup salsa instead of the tomato sauce and substitute tortillas for hamburger buns. Serve on top of hamburger buns.

Make-Ahead
Cheese-and-Hamburger Casserole
Serves 8

1 pound ground beef
1 small onion, chopped
3 cloves garlic, pressed
1 pkg. (8 oz) mushrooms, sliced
   (optional)
6 tablespoons tomato paste (put
   rest of can in a freezer bag and
   mark)
1 teaspoon honey
1 teaspoon thyme
1 teaspoon oregano
salt and pepper to taste

1 (28-ounce) can whole tomatoes
   un-drained and chopped
⅓ cup flour
2 tablespoons butter
2½ cups milk
1 cup crumbled Feta cheese (if
   your kids hate Feta, use
   cheese of your choice)
¾ cup shredded part-skim
   Mozzarella cheese
4 cups uncooked mastacolli
   or similarly shaped pasta

Preheat oven to 350 degrees.
Combine first 3 ingredients in a large skillet, cooking over medium-high heat until browned, stirring to crumble. Salt and pepper to taste. Add mushrooms and cook 5 minutes or until tender. Add tomato paste and next 5 ingredients (tomato paste through whole tomatoes); stir well. Bring mixture to a boil. Then reduce heat and simmer uncovered for 20 minutes. Set aside. Place butter in a medium saucepan and melt over medium heat. Add flour and make into a thick roux. Gradually add milk, whisking until well-blended. Cook for 10 minutes or until thick, stirring constantly. Add cheeses and cook 3 minutes or until cheese melts, stirring constantly. Reserve ½ cup cheese sauce. Pour remaining cheese sauce, beef mixture, and pasta into a 13 X 9-inch baking dish, and stir gently. Drizzle reserved cheese sauce over pasta mixture. Cover and refrigerate 24 hours before baking. Bake at 350 degrees, covered, for an hour or until thoroughly heated through and pasta is tender.

PER SERVING: 493 CALORIES (KCAL); 20G TOTAL FAT; (37% CALORIES FROM FAT); 27G PROTEIN; 51G CARBOHYDRATE; 72MG CHOLESTEROL; 480MG SODIUM. FOOD EXCHANGES: 2½ GRAIN(STARCH); 2½ LEAN MEAT; 2 VEGETABLE; 0 FRUIT; 2½ FAT; 0 OTHER CARBOHYDRATES

Tex-Mex Stuffed Shells

Serves 6

18 uncooked jumbo pasta shells
1 (32 oz.) can tomato sauce
¼ cup oatmeal
2 teaspoons chili powder
1 teaspoon ground cumin
½ pound extra-lean ground beef
1 small onion, chopped
4 sprigs cilantro, coarsely chopped
1 (4 oz.) can chopped green
   chilies, drained
1 (15 oz.) can pinto beans, drained
1 cup Mozzarella cheese, shredded

Preheat oven to 350 degrees. Cook and drain pasta shells as directed on package. While pasta is cooking, mix tomato sauce with chili powder and cumin, set aside. Cook ground beef and onion in 2-quart saucepan over medium heat until beef is browned. Drain and add oatmeal while still hot. Then stir in cilantro, green chilies and pinto beans. Pour 1 cup of the seasoned sauce into a 9 x 13-inch baking dish. Spoon approximately 1½ tablespoons beef mixture into each pasta shell. Place filled sides of the shells up to reveal the inside of each shell and then pour remaining seasoned tomato sauce over shells. Sprinkle with shredded mozzarella cheese. Cover and bake 30 minutes. Let stand uncovered 10 minutes before serving.

PER SERVING: 280 CALORIES (KCAL); 5G TOTAL FAT; (15% CALORIES FROM FAT); 15G PROTEIN; 47G CARBOHYDRATE; 10MG CHOLESTEROL; 1326MG SODIUM. FOOD EXCHANGES: 2 GRAIN(STARCH); 1 LEAN MEAT; 2½ VEGETABLE; 0 FRUIT; ½ FAT; 0 OTHER CARBOHYDRATES

TASTE TESTER COMMENTS:

"I used 9 manicotti shells because I couldn't find the jumbo pasta shell at the grocery. This was a hit! I'm going to keep a batch in the freezer. I can't believe that a ½ pound of ground beef easily filled my family of five. I know this was delicious because my toughest critic brought the 2 leftover manicottis to work the next day!"
Cost per Serving $ 0.91

Double Cheeseburger Pie

Serves 6

2 medium onions, chopped
½ cup oatmeal
¾ pound of ground beef
salt and pepper to taste
1½ cups milk
3 large eggs
¾ cup pancake mix (I use whole wheat pancake mix)
1 cup shredded Cheddar cheese

2 tablespoons butter
2½ cups milk
1 cup crumbled Feta cheese (if your kids hate Feta, use cheese of your choice)
¾ cup shredded part-skim Mozzarella cheese
4 cups uncooked mostaccioli or similarly shaped pasta

Preheat oven to 400 degrees. Lightly grease a 9-inch pie pan. Brown beef, onion and seasoning in large skillet. Pour beef mixture into strainer to drain off any fat. Add oatmeal while still hot. Spread browned beef mixture into pie plate. In a mixing bowl, whisk together milk, eggs and pancake mix until well-blended. Then pour over the ground beef already in the pie plate. Bake for approximately 25 minutes. Carefully remove pie from oven and top with cheese while hot. Bake another 5 minutes longer or until knife poked in center of pie comes out clean. Cool 5 minutes before digging in!

PER SERVING: 324 CALORIES (KCAL); 15G TOTAL FAT; (40% CALORIES FROM FAT); 24G PROTEIN; 24G CARBOHYDRATE; 139MG CHOLESTEROL; 463MG SODIUM. FOOD EXCHANGES: 1 GRAIN(STARCH); 2½ LEAN MEAT; ½ VEGETABLE; 0 FRUIT; 1½ FAT; 0 OTHER CARBOHYDRATES

TASTE TESTER COMMENTS:

"'Mom, tell her this is a WINNER!' Need I say more? We all loved this one. I'm thinking that this would be a great freezer meal. I wouldn't change a thing, delicious!"
Cost per serving: $ 0.52

South of the Border Pizzas

Serves 4

½ pound extra lean ground beef
1 medium onion, chopped
1 teaspoon cumin (I use more)
2 teaspoons garlic powder
4 (10 inch) flour tortillas (I use sprouted whole wheat)
1 medium tomato, seeded and chopped
1 cup mozzarella, shredded

Preheat oven to 400 degrees. Brown ground beef and onion in skillet, and drain well when done. Stir all seasonings into beef. Lightly brush tortillas with oil or use a non-aerosol sprayer. Bake tortillas right on the oven rack for about two minutes. Really watch them—they can burn easily. Spoon beef mixture evenly over top of each tortilla; top with an equal amount of tomato. Sprinkle with cheese. Return to oven and bake 10 minutes or until tortillas are lightly browned. Serve with salsa, sour cream, cilantro or just as they are when they come out of the oven.

PER SERVING: 469 CALORIES (KCAL); 20G TOTAL FAT; (38% CALORIES FROM FAT); 26G PROTEIN; 46G CARBOHYDRATE; 54MG CHOLESTEROL; 535MG SODIUM. FOOD EXCHANGES: 2½ GRAIN(STARCH); 2½ LEAN MEAT; ½ VEGETABLE; 0 FRUIT; 2½ FAT; 0 OTHER CARBOHYDRATES

TASTE TESTER COMMENTS:

"These were awesome! We had salsa with them. I loved how the tortillas came out in the oven. My son licked his plate clean. I guess your next book needs to be on table manners!"

Meatball Soup

Serves 6

1 pound ground beef
½ cup bread crumbs
⅓ cup grated Romano cheese, divided
3 teaspoons oregano, divided
salt and pepper to taste
3 cans beef broth (or equivalent of homemade)
1 (28 oz.) can Italian-style tomatoes
6 carrots, diced
4 medium potatoes, peeled and diced
2 small onions, chopped
6 large garlic cloves, chopped
2 teaspoons thyme

Combine ground beef, bread crumbs, half the grated Romano cheese, 1 teaspoon oregano, salt and pepper to taste in large bowl and blend well. Wet your hands and shape mixture into little meatballs, about an inch in diameter. In a Dutch oven, heat one tablespoon of the oil over medium high heat. Cook onions, garlic and carrots till soft, about 3 minutes. Add beef broth to the Dutch oven and bring to a boil over high heat. Drop in the meatballs and cook 5 minutes. Add canned tomatoes, thyme and remaining 2 teaspoons oregano. Reduce heat to medium. Simmer soup uncovered until meatballs and vegetables are cooked through and tender, breaking up tomatoes with back of spoon, about 40 minutes. Season to taste with salt and pepper. Ladle soup into bowls. Sprinkle with remaining Romano cheese and serve.

PER SERVING: 388 CALORIES (KCAL); 14G TOTAL FAT; (32% CALORIES FROM FAT); 25G PROTEIN; 41G CARBOHYDRATE; 52MG CHOLESTEROL; 947MG SODIUM. FOOD EXCHANGES: 1½ GRAIN(STARCH); 2½ LEAN MEAT; 3 VEGETABLE; 0 FRUIT; 1½ FAT; 0 OTHER CARBOHYDRATES

Mexican Meatball Soup

Serves 8

Hey, I'm on a roll here with these meatballs. Sorry...that was bad. Albondigas is Spanish for meatballs, but Mexican Meatball Soup is easier to say. This soup isn't completely authentic anyway, but it's flavorful enough for both adults and kids to love it!

2 tablespoons olive oil
3 onions, chopped, divided
4 garlic cloves, pressed, divided
1 small bay leaf
5 cans beef broth (or the equivalent of homemade)
1 28-ounce can diced tomatoes (un-drained)
½ cup jarred salsa (your favorite temperature)
½ cup cilantro, chopped—leaves and stems, divided
1 pound lean ground beef
5 tablespoons yellow cornmeal
¼ cup milk
1 large egg
salt and pepper to taste
2 teaspoons ground cumin
2 teaspoons garlic powder
½ cup brown rice

Heat oil in a Dutch oven on a medium-high heat. Add most of the onions (reserve 1 cup for meatballs), 2 garlic cloves and bay leaf, cooking for about 3 minutes until onion is soft. Add broth, tomatoes with juice, salsa and ¼ cup cilantro and bring to a boil. Cover and simmer 15 minutes. Meanwhile, combine ground beef, cornmeal, milk, egg, salt, pepper, cumin, then remaining onions, 2 garlic cloves and remaining cilantro in medium bowl. Mix well. Shape meat mixture into little meatballs (about an inch in diameter), using wet hands. Add brown rice and meatballs to soup and bring to a boil, stirring occasionally. Reduce heat, cover and simmer until rice and meatballs are tender, stirring occasionally, about 30 minutes. Season to taste with salt and pepper. Ladle soup into bowls and serve.

PER SERVING: 326 CALORIES (KCAL); 15G TOTAL FAT; (40% CALORIES FROM FAT); 22G PROTEIN; 27G CARBOHYDRATE; 63MG CHOLESTEROL; 934MG SODIUM. FOOD EXCHANGES: 1 GRAIN(STARCH); 2½ LEAN MEAT; 2 VEGETABLE; 0 FRUIT; 2 FAT; 0 OTHER CARBOHYDRATES

Stuffed Shirts

Serves 4

These hamburgers are really like mini meatloaves with veggies throughout. Kids might balk at first, but give them a try. They are so flavorful and delicious—you may make converts out of them yet!

1 small onion, chopped fine
1 small tomato, finely diced
½ green pepper, finely diced
1 teaspoon dried oregano
1 shot of ketchup
salt and pepper to taste
1 pound lean ground beef
1 egg

In a medium bowl, combine the garlic, diced onion, tomato, green bell pepper, and oregano. Add the salt and pepper, and mix well. Cover with plastic wrap and set aside. In a large bowl, combine the ground beef, egg, ketchup, salt and pepper. Shape into 8 patties. Place a spoonful of the vegetable filling in the center of one patty, top with a second patty, press down firmly, and shape into a round, carefully sealing the sides by gently pinching them together. Repeat with the remaining patties. In a large skillet, brown the hamburgers for about 5 minutes on each side, or until cooked. Serve on buns with all the fixin's. Mmm, mmm.

PER SERVING: 301 CALORIES (KCAL); 21G TOTAL FAT; (62% CALORIES FROM FAT); 23G PROTEIN; 5G CARBOHYDRATE; 125MG CHOLESTEROL; 107MG SODIUM. FOOD EXCHANGES: 0 GRAIN (STARCH); 3½ LEAN MEAT; ½ VEGETABLE; 0 FRUIT; 2 FAT; 0 OTHER CARBOHYDRATES

TASTE TESTER COMMENTS:

"This was a surprising hit even with my non-veggie eating, pickier than picky son!" Cost .98 per serving.

Cottage Pie
Serves 6

The English call Shepherd's Pie, Cottage Pie. I like that. In my first book, *Healthy Foods*, I had two Shepherds' Pies. This time around, I have this one—and it's quite English, if I do say so myself.

2 cups leftover mashed potatoes (or make them, if need be)
2 tablespoons butter
½ pound mushrooms, sliced
1 pound lean ground beef
1 small onion, chopped
4 garlic cloves, pressed
salt and pepper to taste
2 tablespoons flour (I use whole wheat pastry)
¾ cup leftover beef gravy (or make some)
1 medium carrot, sliced
½ cup petite peas
½ teaspoon thyme
1 tablespoon Worcestershire sauce

Preheat oven to 350 degrees. Melt two tablespoons butter in a large skillet over medium-high heat. Add mushrooms and sauté until tender, about 5 minutes. Transfer mushrooms to bowl. Add beef, onion and garlic to the same skillet and cook over medium-high heat until beef is brown. Salt and pepper to taste. Add flour and stir 2 minutes. Add the cooked mushrooms, gravy, carrot, Worcestershire and thyme. Simmer 4 minutes, stirring occasionally. Add peas and mix to incorporate. Spoon beef mixture into an 8-inch square baking dish. Spoon mashed potatoes over the top like you're frosting a cake. Bake until potatoes are heated through and browned, about 25 minutes. Let stand 5 minutes before serving.

PER SERVING: 327 CALORIES (KCAL); 19G TOTAL FAT; (52% CALORIES FROM FAT); 19G PROTEIN; 20G CARBOHYDRATE; 65MG CHOLESTEROL; 460MG SODIUM. FOOD EXCHANGES: 1 GRAIN(STARCH); 2 LEAN MEAT; 1 VEGETABLE; 0 FRUIT; 2½ FAT; 0 OTHER CARBOHYDRATES

TASTE TESTER COMMENTS
"YES! I'll be making this one again. My dad is English and he thought it was wonderful!"
Cost per serving, .89

Son of Manic Meatloaf

Serves 12

Manic Meatloaf was a huge hit in my first book, *Healthy Foods*. I almost never considered doing another meatloaf—why mess with perfection? This one, however, is dang close. Enjoy!

1 cup dried stuffing mix, any kind will do (or make your own with
    dried bread and lots of poultry seasoning, etc.)
1 large egg, beaten
1 cup buttermilk
1½ pounds ground beef
2 teaspoon garlic powder
1 teaspoon thyme
salt and pepper to taste
½ cup ketchup
1 teaspoon honey
1 tablespoon Worcestershire sauce

In a small bowl, mix stuffing mix, egg and buttermilk. Let sit for 10 minutes. Meanwhile, in a larger bowl, place remaining ingredients. Add stuffing mix combo and mix all ingredients well with clean hands. You can ask a child to do this if he can get his hands clean enough! (I hate touching this stuff, but it's great fun for kids). Shape into a huge blimp in a 13 x 9 inch baking dish, and cook at 375 degrees for about an hour.

PER SERVING: 198 CALORIES (KCAL); 8G TOTAL FAT; (38% CALORIES FROM FAT); 13G PROTEIN; 17G CARBOHYDRATE; 44MG CHOLESTEROL; 433MG SODIUM. FOOD EXCHANGES: 1 GRAIN (STARCH); 1½ LEAN MEAT; 0 VEGETABLE; 0 FRUIT; 1 FAT; ½ OTHER CARBOHYDRATES

TASTE TESTER COMMENTS:

"I still like Manic Meatloaf better, but you're right—this is a close second!"

Mighty Mini-Meaty Loaves
Serves 6

This version of meatloaf takes much less time to cook because of the size—plus having your own individual meatloaf makes a kid feel like a grown-up.

1 egg
¾ cup buttermilk
1 cup cheddar cheese, shredded
½ cup oats
1 onion, chopped
1 teaspoon thyme
1 teaspoon cumin
1 teaspoon garlic powder
salt and pepper to taste
1 pound lean ground beef
⅓ cup ketchup
1 tablespoon Worcestershire sauce
2 teaspoons rice wine vinegar

Preheat oven to 350 degrees. Lightly grease a muffin tin.
In a bowl, beat the egg and buttermilk, stir in the cheese, oats, onion and spices. Add beef and mix well. Fill muffin wells, making individual loaves. Combine ketchup, vinegar and Worcestershire sauce and spoon over mini loaves. Bake for 30 to 40 minutes, or until done.

PER SERVING: 198 CALORIES (KCAL); 8G TOTAL FAT; (38% CALORIES FROM FAT); 13G PROTEIN; 17G CARBOHYDRATE; 44MG CHOLESTEROL; 433MG SODIUM. FOOD EXCHANGES: 1 GRAIN (STARCH); 1½ LEAN MEAT; 0 VEGETABLE; 0 FRUIT; 1 FAT; ½ OTHER CARBOHYDRATES

TASTE TESTER COMMENTS:
"I like the little loaves! Great idea. My kids loved this one."
Cost per serving, .86

Chapter 3
CHICKEN
EVERY WHICH WAY

What could be more tragic than to miss out on a good sale on chicken? Why I get positively giddy loading my cart with .69/pound whole chickens. There is an important principle behind a whole chicken vs. a cut-up one: it's cheaper. Not only that, it is the foundation to Rubber Chicken—stretching one poor, pathetic chicken into 3 meals. Rubber Chicken was in my first book, *Healthy Food's*, but bears repeating because it's a real eye opener on how much we can do with one measly chicken. The soup recipe for Day 3 is different than *Healthy Food's*.

Day 1

Roast your chicken. Rinse your bird and pat dry. Sprinkle with salt, pepper and garlic powder. Bake approximately 30 minutes per pound, until juices run clear. Remove chicken from the pan and make gravy. You can stuff your chicken or not. I don't because I am not interested in a big production—just an easy meal. Serve with the usual fixin's – mashed potatoes & plenty of veggies. Remember - you want leftover chicken.

Day 2

"Pick every last ever-lovin' bit of chicken off them bones." Open one 15 oz. can of black beans or pintos (or use homemade beans) and toss the chicken and beans together in a pot. Add 1 tsp. cumin, 1 tsp. garlic powder and some jarred salsa to taste. Warm some flour tortillas and make burritos. Add some shredded cheese, more salsa and you've got dinner!

Day 3

By now, that chicken is in pretty sorry shape. But not to worry—let's make soup! In a large pot, put the chicken carcass, an uncut onion, carrot and celery rib, and cover with cold water. Simmer the daylights out of it— about 1½ hours. Strain broth, discard chicken and now you can make whatever soup you like. Here's a recipe that will bring out the penny pincher in you:

Clean out the Crisper
Vegetable Soup

Serves 6

You've cleaned off the chicken, now let's clean out the crisper.

Chop what you have and set aside (some good options are carrots, celery, cabbage, zucchini, turnips, etc.)
1 small onion chopped
1 can diced tomatoes
1 tsp. garlic powder
1 tsp. thyme
salt and pepper to taste

In a soup pot, sauté the onion till almost clear. Add the rest of the vegetables and cook about 2 minutes. Add the chicken broth (you just made) and seasonings. Let simmer till vegetables are tender and serve with plenty of bread and butter. Rubber Chicken is the gold standard of inexpensive cooking. One chicken equals three meals. Who knew?

Autumn Chicken Breasts

Serves 4

4 skinless boneless chicken breasts
1 tablespoon honey
¼ teaspoon ground cinnamon
1 teaspoon sage
2 medium tart apples, peeled and cut into thin slices
1 cup apple cider or apple juice
1 tablespoon cornstarch

Preheat oven to 350 degrees. Place chicken breast halves between 2 pieces of waxed paper and pound chicken to about a □ inch thickness. Brown chicken in a skillet heated with a little olive oil. Remove to plate and set aside covered to keep from drying out. Mix honey, sage and cinnamon together and coat apple slices in this cinnamon mixture. Divide apple slices among chicken breast halves. Fold chicken around apples and secure with toothpicks. Place chicken in a 13 X 9 baking dish and bake for 20 minutes or until done. Mix apple cider with the cornstarch till smooth and add to the skillet in which the chicken was originally cooked. Cook over medium heat using a wire whisk to get up any bits from the pan, stirring constantly, until thickened and bubbly. Spoon over the baked chicken and serve.

PER SERVING: 344 CALORIES (KCAL); 3G TOTAL FAT; (8% CALORIES FROM FAT); 55G PROTEIN; 22G CARBOHYDRATE; 137MG CHOLESTEROL; 157MG SODIUM. FOOD EXCHANGES: 0 GRAIN (STARCH); 7½ LEAN MEAT; 0 VEGETABLE; 1 FRUIT; 0 FAT; ½ OTHER CARBOHYDRATES

TASTE TESTER COMMENTS:

"This smelled wonderful while cooking and everyone loved it though I admit, I wasn't so sure about the apple part. I will definitely make this again!"
Cost per serving .79

Roast Chicken with Herbed Butter

Serves 8

5 tablespoons butter, softened
1 tablespoon fresh chopped parsley
1 teaspoon thyme, dried
1 teaspoon rosemary, dried and crushed
¼ teaspoon fennel seeds, crushed
½ cup dry white wine
1½ teaspoons flour

salt and pepper to taste
1 great big, roasting chicken, rinsed, patted dry
3 medium onions, peeled and quartered
14 garlic cloves, peeled
1 cup chicken broth (canned or otherwise)

Mix butter, chopped herbs, fennel seeds and salt and pepper in bowl, blending well. Preheat oven to 400 degrees. Starting at the neck end, slide fingers under skin of breast and upper part of legs, loosening the chicken's skin. Spread 3 tablespoons of the herb butter under the skin of the breast and of the upper leg meat. Place chicken on rack in large roasting pan. A lot of people use kitchen string and tie the legs together, but I skip that step in favor of just getting the thing in the oven. Put the onions around your buttered bird. Season liberally with salt and plenty of freshly ground pepper. Roast chicken 30 minutes. Add garlic cloves to pan and brush the chicken with some of the reserved herb butter. Roast until the chicken is golden brown and a meat thermometer reaches 180 degrees when inserted into the thickest part of the thigh. Sometimes, I'll flip the bird if it looks like it's getting too browned. That also helps the juices run to the breast, keeping it juicier. To do this, use a wooden spoon inserted into the cavity and a clean oven mitt that you don't mind getting dirty. That's how I do it anyway—but you do it your way and for heaven's sake, be safe. When the chicken is finished, remove from the pan and set on a plate. Set the roasting pan over medium-high heat and add broth and wine; bring to simmer, scraping up browned bits. Remove any visible fat with a spoon. Pour juices into medium saucepan. Stir reserved 1 tablespoon herb butter and flour in small bowl to smooth paste. Bring pan juices to a simmer; and whisk in the butter-flour paste. Simmer sauce until slightly thickened, whisking almost constantly, about 4 minutes. Correct the seasoning with salt and pepper: Serve chicken with sauce. Killer chicken.

PER SERVING: 370 CALORIES (KCAL); 27G TOTAL FAT; (67% CALORIES FROM FAT); 23G PROTEIN; 6G CARBOHYDRATE; 109MG CHOLESTEROL; 255MG SODIUM. FOOD EXCHANGES: 0 GRAIN(STARCH); 3 LEAN MEAT; 1 VEGETABLE; 0 FRUIT; 3½ FAT; 0 OTHER CARBOHYDRATES

Fragrant Lemon Chicken and Potatoes

Serves 6

This chicken needs to marinate, so do this the night before you plan on serving it or in the morning of the day you plan to serve it.

1 chicken, quartered
6 potatoes, peeled and quartered
6 garlic cloves, pressed
1 can chicken broth
⅓ cup olive oil
⅓ cup fresh lemon juice
2 teaspoons oregano, crumbled

Whisk olive oil, lemon juice, garlic and oregano to combine. In a large zipper bag, place chicken and potatoes and pour mixture over the top. Mush around to distribute and place in the refrigerator. Move it around from time to time, when you remember. Preheat oven to 375 degrees. Place chicken mixture in a 13 X 9 baking pan, salt and pepper to taste, then bake until chicken is cooked through and potatoes are tender, basting occasionally, about 1 hour 15 minutes. Serve with steamed broccoli and baby carrots.

PER SERVING: 402 CALORIES (KCAL); 24G TOTAL FAT; (54% CALORIES FROM FAT); 26G PROTEIN; 20G CARBOHYDRATE; 98MG CHOLESTEROL; 174MG SODIUM. FOOD EXCHANGES: 1 GRAIN(STARCH); 3½ LEAN MEAT; 0 VEGETABLE; 0 FRUIT; 3 FAT; 0 OTHER CARBOHYDRATES

TASTE TESTER COMMENTS:

"One of my favorite flavors is lemon with chicken and this was absolutely delicious. I think it had a lot to do with marinating it the night before—it really was good. I will make this often!"
Cost per serving...79

Chicken with 40 Cloves of Garlic

Serves 8

2 medium onions, chopped
1 teaspoon tarragon
6 sprigs of parsley
4 celery stalks, cut into three
   pieces each
8 chicken thighs, skinned
8 chicken drumsticks, skinned

½ cup vermouth, or juice or
   stock-whatever you have on
   hand
salt and pepper to taste
dash of nutmeg
4 heads of garlic, separated into
   cloves (about 40 cloves)

Combine first 4 ingredients in a 4-quart casserole. Arrange chicken over vegetables. Drizzle with vermouth; sprinkle with salt, pepper, and nutmeg. Nestle garlic around chicken. Cover casserole with aluminum foil, then casserole lid. Bake at 375 degrees for 1½ hours.

PER SERVING: 192 CALORIES (KCAL); 5G TOTAL FAT; (25% CALORIES FROM FAT); 24G PROTEIN; 7G CARBOHYDRATE; 86MG CHOLESTEROL; 137MG SODIUM. FOOD EXCHANGES: 0 GRAIN(STARCH); 3 LEAN MEAT; 1 VEGETABLE; 0 FRUIT; 0 FAT; 0 OTHER CARBOHYDRATES

TASTE TESTERS COMMENTS:

"I enjoyed it and 6 year old Molly, our non-adventurous eater, gave it 2 thumbs up
(with a mouth full of chicken) 4 year old Kacey added,
'The chicken! Yes, it is good!'"
Cost per serving .97

Chicken Marengo

Serves 6

This classic bistro dish was actually served to Napoleon after the battle of Marengo. History and great chicken—who can beat it?

1 whole chicken, cut into pieces	1 (8 oz.) can diced tomatoes
4 cloves of garlic, pressed	1 tablespoon tomato paste
2 tablespoons olive oil	½ small onion, thinly sliced
1 small onion, chopped	1 tablespoon butter
¼ teaspoon thyme	½ pound mushrooms, thinly
salt and pepper to taste	sliced
½ cup white wine	¾ cup black olives, pitted
½ lemon, juiced	

In a Dutch oven, sauté the chopped onions and garlic in olive oil until lightly browned. Then remove onions and garlic, and reserve. In the same pot brown the chicken. Mix together tomato paste and chopped tomatoes, stir in wine, browned onions and garlic, and seasonings. Top chicken pieces with liquid mixture. Cover tightly and simmer for 30 to 45 minutes—watch your pan! As the chicken is simmering, in a separate skillet sauté the remaining onion slices and mushrooms in butter until golden. Add olives and lemon juice to the mixture. Then pour this mixture over the top of the chicken in the Dutch oven and cover. Cook another 15 - 20 minutes. If you're smart, you'll double this recipe and freeze it for another time. The flavor just gets better!

PER SERVING: 122 CALORIES (KCAL); 7G TOTAL FAT; (52% CALORIES FROM FAT); 8G PROTEIN; 6G CARBOHYDRATE; 20MG CHOLESTEROL; 166MG SODIUM. FOOD EXCHANGES: 0 GRAIN(STARCH); 1 LEAN MEAT; 1 VEGETABLE; 0 FRUIT; 1 FAT; 0 OTHER CARBOHYDRATES

TASTE TESTER COMMENTS:

"My husband HATES olives with a passion, but I never told him they were in this dish. I simply took them out of his portion. He thought this was completely wonderful and said we couldn't have done better going out! Now THAT'S a compliment. Kids were equally as enthusiastic as long as the olives remained a mystery—I ate every one of them!"
Cost per serving .94

CHICKEN DISSECTION 101

It's really a snap to cut up a chicken. Why pay up to $2.00 more a pound to have someone do it for you? If you have kitchen scissors, the job is even easier. Here's how to do it:

1. Place chicken breast side up on your cutting board. Take your scissors and cut the loose skin between the thigh and breast.

2. Holding one leg with each hand, bend both legs toward the back till the bones break at the hip joints.

3. Remove the leg and thigh from the body by cutting with a knife between the joints, keeping the knife close to the bones.

4. Locate the joint between the thigh and leg and cut through with the knife.

5. Remove wings by placing chicken on its back and cutting the inside of the wing, just over the joint. Pull the wing away and cut down through the joint (you can use your scissors for this task).

6. To separate the breast, place chicken on its neck cavity and cut down toward the board, following along the side of the rib cage.

7. Remember to clean the board with a bleach solution to kill all cooties, when you are done.

Turkey Tetrazzini
Serves 6

Believe it or not, this recipe has been thinned down substantially. The portions aren't large. If you add a huge salad to your dinner table and some steamed veggies, you'll balance out. As long as you're not eating high fat food every night, it's okay to enjoy a treat like this every once in awhile. Especially when there's a leftover turkey in your fridge that needs dealing with!

¼ cup butter, divided	1 tablespoon olive oil
¼ cup flour	3 cloves garlic, pressed
3½ cups chicken broth	6 green onions, thinly sliced
½ cup sherry	¼ cup parsley, chopped fine
½ cup milk	½ pound mushrooms, thinly sliced
½ teaspoon oregano	1 pound spaghetti
¼ cup Romano cheese	2 cups cooked turkey, chopped
	salt and pepper to taste

Melt □ cup butter in a heavy saucepan. Stir in flour and cook 1 to 2 minutes, but do not brown. Add broth, sherry, milk, and oregano. Cook, stirring constantly, until sauce comes to a boil. Add ¼ cup Romano cheese, stirring until melted. Remove from heat and set aside. Melt remaining butter with oil in skillet. Add garlic, scallions, parsley, and mushrooms and sauté until mushrooms are brown. Remove from heat. Cook spaghetti according to package directions until al dente. Drain well. Combine sauce, mushrooms, spaghetti, and turkey; season with salt and pepper to taste. Pour into greased casserole and sprinkle with remaining cheese. Bake at 375 degrees for 15 minutes, or until bubbly.

PER SERVING: 430 CALORIES (KCAL); 11G TOTAL FAT; (24% CALORIES FROM FAT); 27G PROTEIN; 50G CARBOHYDRATE; 58MG CHOLESTEROL; 480MG SODIUM. FOOD EXCHANGES: 3 GRAIN (STARCH); 2 LEAN MEAT; ½ VEGETABLE; 0 FRUIT; 1½ FAT; 0 OTHER CARBOHYDRATES

TASTE TESTER COMMENTS:
"My mother-in-law makes the REALLY high fat version of this (she uses heavy cream!) and it's divine. I thought this version was just as good and I didn't feel so weighed down. Thanks for the recipe!" Cost per serving .78

Alice Johnston's Thanksgiving Pie

Serves 4 to 6

Alice Johnston is my best friend Sharon Johnston's mother-in-law and is the best of the best when it comes to great, quick, family cooking. Alice's Thanksgiving Pie shows her ingenuity and a quick and easy way to use up those Thanksgiving leftovers! The portions are not specified in this recipe, but eyeball your pie pan and prepare accordingly. Obviously, if you don't have enough of anything, add something else or skip it entirely. The idea here isn't to make a bunch of work, but to use up your good leftovers before they become science project candidates in the fridge.

Leftover turkey, chopped
Leftover gravy, heated
Leftover stuffing
Leftover potatoes
Leftover veggies
Leftover cranberries

Preheat oven to 375 degrees.
In an 8 or 9 inch pie pan, press leftover stuffing in the bottom to make a pie shell of sorts. Next, make a layer of potatoes, then veggies. Add chopped turkey to heated gravy and mix well. Pour into the middle of your "pie" and put it in the oven. Bake for 20 minutes or so until completely heated through. Serve with leftover cranberries.

TASTE TESTER'S COMMENTS:
"When I first saw my mother-in-law making this I have to admit, I had my reservations. But it was wonderful and now I do this every year with my leftovers." Cost per serving: FREE (since we paid on Thanksgiving!)

WAY Easy Chicken Stir Fry
Serves 4

1 tablespoon ketchup
1 dash soy sauce, or to taste
2 teaspoons ground ginger, or grate
  some fresh
2 cloves garlic, pressed
3 skinless, boneless chicken breasts,
  sliced thin
1 tablespoon oil
1 tablespoon sesame oil
6 green onions, sliced thick
1 small green pepper, sliced thin
1 small red pepper, sliced thin
4 cups cooked rice (I use brown)

Mix soy sauce, ketchup, ginger and garlic in re-sealable heavy-duty plastic bag. Add chicken; seal bag and turn to coat with marinade. Let stand 15 minutes while you cut up the veggies. Heat 1 tablespoon of the oil in 10-inch skillet or wok over medium-high heat. Add green onions and bell peppers; stir-frying until crisp-tender. Remove from skillet. Heat the remaining 1 tablespoon sesame oil in skillet and add the chicken, quickly stir-frying about 5 minutes or less, until chicken is cooked. Stir in bell pepper mixture. Serve on top of brown rice.

PER SERVING: 430 CALORIES (KCAL); 11G TOTAL FAT; (24% CALORIES FROM FAT); 27G PROTEIN; 50G CARBOHYDRATE; 58MG CHOLESTEROL; 480MG SODIUM. FOOD EXCHANGES: 3 GRAIN(STARCH); 2 LEAN MEAT; ½ VEGETABLE; 0 FRUIT; 1½ FAT; 0 OTHER CARBOHYDRATES

TASTE TESTERS COMMENTS:
"I love these easy chicken recipes!
This was delicious and took me minutes to make. I love that!"
Cost per serving .97

Country Fried Chicken and Peppers

Serves 4

4 boneless skinless chicken breasts
2 tablespoons cornmeal
1 tablespoon flour
1 teaspoon paprika
1 teaspoon garlic powder
1 teaspoon onion powder
salt and pepper to taste
½ teaspoon cumin
1 tablespoon oil
1 small green bell pepper, cut into thin strips
1 small red bell pepper, cut into thin strips

Pound chicken to ¼-inch thickness. Stir together the cornmeal, flour, paprika, garlic salt, onion powder, pepper and cumin. Dip chicken in water; allow excess water to drip off. Then dip into cornmeal mixture, coating both sides well. In large skillet heat olive oil. Cook chicken over medium heat for 4 minutes. Turn over and add pepper strips to skillet. Cook 4 more minutes or until chicken is nicely browned and cooked through. Remove chicken from skillet. Cook peppers 1-2 minutes more if necessary until tender. Serve chicken with cooked peppers.

PER SERVING: 335 CALORIES (KCAL); 7G TOTAL FAT; (18% CALORIES FROM FAT); 56G PROTEIN; 10G CARBOHYDRATE; 137MG CHOLESTEROL; 156MG SODIUM. FOOD EXCHANGES: ½ GRAIN(STARCH); 7½ LEAN MEAT; ½ VEGETABLE; 0 FRUIT; ½ FAT; 0 OTHER CARBOHYDRATES

TASTE TESTERS COMMENTS:

"This was very good and easy and a crowd pleaser for everyone but the baby! Thanks again!"
Cost per serving .98

Very Garlic-y Chicken Caesar Salad

Serves 4

3 to 4 ounces of chicken per person (use whatever you have on hand—leftovers are fine or you can grill some)
1 head romaine lettuce, chopped
generous handful of croutons (make your own with stale bread—recipe included)
2-3 cloves garlic, pressed
2 teaspoons lemon juice
½ teaspoon Dijon mustard
1 (2 ounce) can anchovy fillets, drained
¼ cup grated Romano cheese (I use Romano over Parmesan because it's stronger and you can use less)
2 tablespoons red wine vinegar
⅓ cup olive oil
1 teaspoon Worcestershire sauce
salt and pepper to taste

Make croutons by chopping up stale bread, brushing with olive oil and sprinkling with garlic powder. Toast in 350 degree oven till brown—probably no more than 10 minutes. Check them often, though! Wash romaine and chop into bite-sized pieces. Normally, you only want to tear lettuce, but if you are going to be serving it quickly—chop away and save yourself some time. In a bowl, combine oil, vinegar, Worcestershire, salt and pepper to taste, garlic, lemon juice, anchovies and mustard. Or use your food processor. (that's what I do) In a large bowl, toss lettuce and dressing and half the cheese together, along with your tasty croutons. Serve on individual plates and top with your chicken and remaining cheese. Perfect dinner on hot summer nights.

PER SERVING: 286 CALORIES (KCAL); 17G TOTAL FAT; (53% CALORIES FROM FAT); 25G PROTEIN; 9G CARBOHYDRATE; 55MG CHOLESTEROL; 669MG SODIUM. FOOD EXCHANGES: 0 GRAIN(STARCH); 3 LEAN MEAT; 1 VEGETABLE; 0 FRUIT; 3 FAT; 0 OTHER CARBOHYDRATES

TASTE TESTER COMMENTS:

"We tried your Garlick-y Chicken Salad tonight for dinner and everyone liked it! The children actually cleaned their plates. I was surprised because new dishes are usually greeted with complaint."
Cost per serving: .99

Tex-Mex Chicken Soup

Serves 6

I know what you're thinking...what are split peas doing in this? Well, they add body to the soup and you're just going to have to trust me on this. You will love it!

2 teaspoons chili powder
2 teaspoons cumin
salt and pepper to taste
1 teaspoon garlic powder
¼ teaspoon cayenne pepper
  (or less if you're timid)
1 pound chicken breasts,
  skinned and boned (I use
  those frozen boneless breasts)
1 tablespoon olive oil
1 large onion, sliced

1 small bell pepper, sliced
2 cups chicken broth
2 cups water
½ cup split peas
salt and pepper to taste
½ cup jarred salsa
1 tablespoon lime juice
3 corn tortillas, cut into
  ¼-inch wide strips
¾ cup jack cheese

Combine the first 6 ingredients in a shallow dish. Dredge the chicken in the spice mixture. Heat olive oil in a large skillet over medium-high heat. Add the chicken, and sauté 6 minutes on each side or until chicken is done. Remove chicken from pan, and cool. Cut the chicken into ½-inch pieces. Add onions and bell pepper to the skillet and sauté for 3 minutes. Add broth, water, split peas, and salt and pepper to taste. Bring to a boil. Partially cover, reduce heat, and simmer for 30 minutes or until the peas are tender. Add chicken, salsa and lime juice, and simmer an additional 10 minutes. Preheat broiler. Spread the tortilla strips in a single layer on a baking sheet coated with olive oil; lightly rub tortillas into oil on baking sheet. Broil tortilla strips 4 minutes or until lightly browned, stirring once. Ladle soup into each of 6 bowls and top with tortilla strips, and sprinkle with cheese.

PER SERVING: 325 CALORIES (KCAL); 9G TOTAL FAT; (26% CALORIES FROM FAT); 38G PROTEIN; 22G CARBOHYDRATE; 81MG CHOLESTEROL; 536MG SODIUM. FOOD EXCHANGES: 1 GRAIN(STARCH); 4½ LEAN MEAT; ½ VEGETABLE; 0 FRUIT; 1 FAT; 0 OTHER CARBOHYDRATE; 81MG CHOLESTEROL; 536MG SODIUM. FOOD EXCHANGES: 1 GRAIN(STARCH); 4½ LEAN MEAT; ½ VEGETABLE; 0 FRUIT; 1 FAT; 0 CARBOHYDRATES

TASTE TESTER COMMENTS:

"I loved this! It was slightly green but I didn't care! I would add sour cream and chopped cilantro on the top for a great meal."
Cost per serving: .90

Saucy Salsa Cornmeal Coated ☆ Chicken ☆

Serves 7

2 ½ pounds cut up chicken
(or do it yourself – see sidebar, page 43)
2 tablespoons cornmeal
salt and pepper to taste
½ teaspoon chili powder
1 teaspoon garlic powder
¼ teaspoon oregano
2 tablespoons butter
2 tablespoons olive oil
Saucy Salsa Sauce (see recipe below)

SAUCY SALSA SAUCE:
1 medium tomato, chopped
1 small onion, chopped
1 clove garlic, pressed
1 jalapeno pepper, seeded and finely chopped (use half this
amount if you're timid)
4 sprigs cilantro, chopped

Heat oven to 375 degrees Cut chicken into pieces; cut each breast half into halves and remove skin. Mix cornmeal, salt, pepper, garlic powder, chili powder and oregano. Coat chicken with cornmeal mixture by pressing mixture firmly into flesh. Meanwhile, heat butter and oil in 13 x 9 inch pan in the oven until butter is melted. Place chicken, meaty sides down, in pan. Bake uncovered 30 minutes. Turn chicken; cook until brown another 20 to 30 minutes longer. Prepare Saucy Salsa Sauce by mixing all ingredients together; serve with chicken.

PER SERVING: 162 CALORIES (KCAL); 10G TOTAL FAT; (58% CALORIES FROM FAT); 13G PROTEIN; 4G CARBOHYDRATE; 39MG CHOLESTEROL; 164MG SODIUM.

TASTE TESTERS COMMENTS:

"I told you I loved new chicken recipes. This was a huge hit with my crew. The baby loved it, too (without the sauce!)."
Cost per serving .89

Caribbean Chicken

Serves 6

5 cloves garlic, pressed
2 jalapeno peppers, seeded and chopped (use gloves)
⅓ cup lemon juice
¼ cup honey
2 teaspoons thyme
6 boneless, skinless chicken breasts

Mix together in a blender all ingredients, except chicken. Pour prepared marinade and chicken into a big ziplock-type plastic bag. Turn chicken around several times to coat with marinade. Refrigerate at least 2 hours (but no longer than 6 hours) mush it around every once in awhile in the fridge.   For best flavor, grill chicken on the barby, turning and brushing frequently with marinade, until the juice of chicken is no longer pink when thickest pieces are cut. Discard any remaining marinade- That's a food poisoning waiting to happen! Don't you go drenching your hot cooked chicken in that stuff for "more flavor" either! You'll make yourself sick! If your grill is covered with snow, use your oven. Preheat to 375 degrees and cook about 45 minutes or until chicken is no longer pink.

PER SERVING: 312 CALORIES (KCAL); 3G TOTAL FAT; (8% CALORIES FROM FAT); 55G PROTEIN; 14G CARBOHYDRATE; 137MG CHOLESTEROL; 155MG SODIUM. FOOD EXCHANGES: 0 GRAIN (STARCH); 7½ LEAN MEAT; 0 VEGETABLE; 0 FRUIT; 0 FAT; 1 OTHER CARBOHYDRATES

TASTE TESTER COMMENTS:

"I think you're making me into a marinade convert! The flavor of this chicken is so good, although a little spicy, but we all loved it!"
Cost per serving .92

Quick Orange Ginger Chicken

Serves 4

2 tablespoons orange juice
1 small onion, chopped
2 cups brown rice
¼ teaspoon thyme leaves
3 tablespoons finely chopped crystallized ginger (found in jars in the ethnic aisle of your grocery store)
4 skinless, boneless chicken breast halves
1 tablespoon orange juice
¼ teaspoon ground ginger

Heat oven to 350 degrees. Heat 1 tablespoon orange juice to boiling in 2-quart saucepan over medium heat. Cook onion in orange juice, stirring frequently for just a few minutes. Stir in rice, chopped ginger, another 1 tablespoon orange juice and the thyme. Spoon rice mixture into a lightly greased 8"square baking dish. Place chicken breasts over rice mixture; brush with 1 tablespoon orange juice; sprinkle liberally with ground ginger. Cover and bake 30 minutes. Remove cover; bake 15 to 20 minutes longer or until juice of chicken is no longer pink when centers of thickest pieces are cut.

PER SERVING: 632 CALORIES (KCAL); 6G TOTAL FAT; (8% CALORIES FROM FAT); 62G PROTEIN; 79G CARBOHYDRATE; 137MG CHOLESTEROL; 160MG SODIUM. FOOD EXCHANGES: 5 GRAIN(STARCH); 7½ LEAN MEAT; ½ VEGETABLE; 0 FRUIT; ½ FAT; 0 OTHER CARBOHYDRATES

TASTE TESTER COMMENTS:

"This was a very simple recipe, once I found the crystallized ginger.
Lots of flavor!"
Cost per serving .99

Roast Chicken and Potatoes

Serves 6

6 skinless, boneless chicken breasts
1 pound small red potatoes, halved or quartered, depending on size
⅓ cup mayonnaise (I use a low-fat mayo)
3 tablespoons Dijon mustard
salt and pepper to taste
1 to 2 teaspoons thyme
3 cloves garlic, pressed
chives, for garnish

Heat oven to 350 degrees. Lightly grease a 13 X 9-inch pan. Place chicken and potatoes in pan. Mix remaining ingredients and brush over chicken and potatoes. Salt and pepper to taste. Bake uncovered 30 to 35 minutes or until potatoes are tender and juice of chicken is no longer pink when centers of thickest pieces are cut. Sprinkle with chives.

PER SERVING: 341 CALORIES (KCAL); 4G TOTAL FAT; (11% CALORIES FROM FAT); 57G PROTEIN; 16G CARBOHYDRATE; 143MG CHOLESTEROL; 320MG SODIUM. FOOD EXCHANGES: 1 GRAIN(STARCH); 7½ LEAN MEAT; 0 VEGETABLE; 0 FRUIT; 0 FAT; 0 OTHER CARBOHYDRATES

TASTE TESTER COMMENTS:
"Another easy recipe that surprised me with how flavorful and good it is!
I can do this!"
Cost per serving .92

Chicken Satay
Serves 8

4 boneless, skinless chicken breasts, sliced into ¼-inch thick strips
4 chicken thighs, boned and skinned, sliced into strips

12 wooden skewers for grilling -soaked in water for one hour (very important!)

SPICED PEANUT SAUCE:

6 cloves garlic, pressed
4 tablespoons ginger, grated
4 green onions, thinly sliced
½ cup cilantro, chopped (using both leaves and stems for best flavor)
4 tablespoons rice vinegar
1 cup dry sherry
½ cup bottled hoi sin sauce

½ cup soy sauce (I prefer low-sodium)
4 teaspoons sesame oil
4 tablespoons creamy peanut butter (use only a natural peanut butter - no hydrogenated oils)
4 teaspoons honey
2 teaspoons crushed red pepper flakes

Mix sauce ingredients thoroughly (I suggest making a double batch, to freeze half for later.) Pour half the marinade over the chicken in a bowl. Reserve the other half for later. Refrigerate. Cover the marinating chicken tightly with plastic wrap and marinate for several hours. Later on, thread chicken onto the skewers and place on a sheet pan in a single layer. To grill: Barbecue the chicken over low coals, basting constantly with leftover marinade to prevent it from drying out. Heat the reserved marinade well to kill any cooties and pour over the chicken and serve.

PER SERVING: 418 CALORIES (KCAL); 15G TOTAL FAT; (33% CALORIES FROM FAT); 39G PROTEIN; 26G CARBOHYDRATE; 98MG CHOLESTEROL; 1011MG SODIUM. FOOD EXCHANGES: ½ GRAIN(STARCH); 5 LEAN MEAT; ½ VEGETABLE; 0 FRUIT; 2 FAT; 1 OTHER CARBOHYDRATES

TASTE TESTER COMMENTS:
"My kids loved this! I was shocked! The idea of putting peanut butter on anything didn't seem like such a good idea, but I loved it as much as the kids. Thanks for this one...we'll make it often!"
Cost per serving .99

Tortilla Soup
Serves 4

1 tablespoon olive oil
1 small onion, chopped
2 garlic cloves, pressed
½ cup packed fresh cilantro, stems and all, chopped
1½ cups cooked chicken, chopped
3½ cups chicken broth
½ cup jarred salsa
4 corn tortillas, cut into strips
1 ripe avocado (optional—only on sale), cut into cubes
2 tablespoons fresh lime juice
½ cup jack cheese, grated

Preheat oven to 400 degrees. Arrange tortilla strips on a cookie sheet then spray lightly with a non-aerosol oil pump. Bake for 5 to 10 minutes till crispy. Watch them—they could burn easily. Ladle into bowls, squeeze in a little lime juice (about a teaspoonful), garnish with tortilla strips, avocado and jack cheese.

PER SERVING: 296 CALORIES (KCAL); 12G TOTAL FAT; (36% CALORIES FROM FAT); 27G PROTEIN; 20G CARBOHYDRATE; 57MG CHOLESTEROL; 974MG SODIUM. FOOD EXCHANGES: 1 GRAIN(STARCH); 3½ LEAN MEAT; 1 VEGETABLE; 0 FRUIT; 1½ FAT; 0 OTHER CARBOHYDRATES

TASTE TESTER COMMENTS:
"Definitely a recipe for the more developed palate – a great way to use the freshest summer ingredients! We added some golden raisins and chopped almonds on top to create a truly gourmet flavor!" Cost per serving: $1.01

Chapter 4
BEANS, BEANS, GOOD FOR YOUR HEART

Probably the one food that most people consider to be the ultimate expression in thrifty living is the lowly bean. Beans may be great for the budget, but they're also a healthy fast food, earning high marks in vitamins, protein and fiber. Not only that, they're wonderfully versatile and easy...perfect for frantic family cooking.

Recently, on one of my bargain scavenger hunts, I came across a clearance table at the market absolutely loaded down with bags of dried beans for a mere .25 a bag. Naturally, I bought them all and have enjoyed trying out new recipes and ideas with them. Not all have been hits, but most have been. Here is a hefty collection of some of my family's favorites.

I must admit to giggling a bit over beans. What other food do you know of that comes with its very own soundtrack? For most people, the "musicality" of beans can be a little embarrassing and inconvenient, to say the least. So how do you get rid of the noise?

The best answer to that, believe it or not, is to build up a tolerance by eating more beans! Not everyone agrees however, and a good friend of mine tells me that a pinch of baking soda in the soak water works to get the "music" out. Another friend swears by throwing a carrot in the soak water. Maybe try all of the above and see what works. Be sure you let me know – we could use a little help at this house!

Twin Bean Casserole

Serves 7

This adapted recipe comes from my realtor twin friends, Joyce and Loyce who sold us our wonderful 125 year old farmhouse.

1 teaspoon olive oil
cooking spray (non aerosol)
1 small onion, chopped
3 clove garlic, pressed
1 (8 oz.) can corn, drained
1 can chopped chilies, drained
½ cup jarred salsa
1 teaspoon cumin
2 (16 oz.) cans pinto beans,
  drained

1 (14.5 oz.) can stewed tomatoes,
  un-drained
1 cup shredded Cheddar cheese,
  divided
¾ cup cornmeal
¼ cup flour
½ teaspoon honey
salt and pepper to taste
½ cup buttermilk
¼ cup olive oil
2 egg whites, lightly beaten

Preheat oven to 375 degrees.
Heat 1 teaspoon olive oil in a large saucepan coated with cooking spray (see notes, page 15) over medium-high heat. Add onion and garlic, and sauté approximately 3 minutes. Add ½ cup corn, ¼ cup chilies and next 4 ingredients (salsa through tomatoes), and bring to a boil. Reduce heat, and simmer 10 minutes. Pour mixture into a lightly greased 13 X 9-inch baking dish and sprinkle with ½ cup cheese; set baking dish aside. Combine cornmeal, flour, honey, and ¼ teaspoon salt in a medium bowl. In another bowl combine ½ cup corn, ¼ cup chilies, ½ cup cheese, buttermilk, ¼ cup oil and the beaten egg whites. Add to cornmeal mixture, stirring just until moist. Spread batter evenly over bean mixture. Bake casserole at 375 degrees for 20-25 minutes or until corn bread is lightly browned.

PER SERVING: 330 CALORIES (KCAL); 11G TOTAL FAT; (28% CALORIES FROM FAT); 15G PROTEIN; 45G CARBOHYDRATE; 4MG CHOLESTEROL; 771MG SODIUM. FOOD EXCHANGES: 2½ GRAIN(STARCH); 1 LEAN MEAT; 1½ VEGETABLE; 0 FRUIT; 1½ FAT; 0 OTHER CARBOHYDRATES

TASTE TESTER COMMENTS:

"My very picky, non-bean eating daughter said: "It smelled so good while baking. This is great. Really a keeper. I can't believe how good it is."
Cost per serving .97

Snappy Black Bean Soup

Serves 12

2 cups black beans, rinsed and soaked
   overnight
2 tablespoons olive oil
1 onion, chopped
2 cloves of garlic, pressed
2 teaspoons cumin
2 cups chicken broth
1 cup jarred salsa

In a crock pot, place your soaked black beans. In a skillet, heat oil and sauté onion and garlic together for 3 minutes or until onion is soft. Add this mixture to the crock pot. Then, add cumin and chicken broth and cook on low all day -about 8 hours. Stir the salsa in just before serving. You can serve this delicious soup topped with sour cream and green onions, if you like.

PER SERVING: 148 CALORIES (KCAL); 3G TOTAL FAT; (18% CALORIES FROM FAT); 8G PROTEIN; 23G CARBOHYDRATE; 0MG CHOLESTEROL; 223MG SODIUM. FOOD EXCHANGES: 1½ GRAIN (STARCH); ½ LEAN MEAT; ½ VEGETABLE; 0 FRUIT; ½ FAT; 0 OTHER CARBOHYDRATES

BEAN BAIL OUT

The only thing required of dried beans that sometimes stops us in our tracks is the preparation. Most beans have to be pre-soaked before they can be used. In a perfect world, this wouldn't be a problem, but for those who live in the real world, we don't always have the forethought to remember to pre-soak the night before bean day. An easy way to combat this perplexing, non-pre-soaked bean problem is to make it a habit of soaking your beans right when you unload them from the grocery bag. In a colander, pick through and rinse the beans as usual and place them in a pot of water (with a good 2 inch clearance of water over the top). Let them sit overnight, drain and put them in a freezer zipper-type bag, date and label them with a Sharpie (the only freezer-friendly pen available—keep it in your zipper bag box to avoid being lifted by the thieves in your house!) and stick them in the freezer. Then, when you are ready to cook with beans, the pre-soak step has already been handled. Or shoot, just open a can and forget about it!

Curried Lentil Soup

Serves 6

This delicious soup was a big hit with my *Healthy Foods* readers!

2 teaspoons olive oil
1 cup chopped onion
1¼ teaspoons curry powder
3 cups water
4 cups chicken broth
3 cups lentils (or use one package—that's what I do)
2 teaspoons basil
2 tablespoons balsamic vinegar
 salt and pepper to taste
1 (14.5-oz.) can diced tomatoes, un-drained

Heat oil in a large Dutch oven over medium-high heat. Add onion and sauté for about 4 minutes. Add curry; sauté another minute. Add water, chicken broth and lentils and bring to a boil. Then cover and reduce heat. Simmer for 40 minutes or until lentils are tender. Or, after the onion is cooked, put everything in a crock-pot and cook on high 3 to 4 hours, or low 7 to 8 hours. But remember, crock-pot times are different because some brands cook hotter than others; so you'll have to check yours out. Place about half the lentil mixture in a blender and process until smooth. Return everything to the pot and add basil, vinegar, salt, and tomatoes cooking until thoroughly heated.

PER SERVING: 388 CALORIES (KCAL); 4G TOTAL FAT; (8% CALORIES FROM FAT); 31G PROTEIN; 61G CARBOHYDRATE; 0MG CHOLESTEROL; 529MG SODIUM. FOOD EXCHANGES: 3½ GRAIN (STARCH); 2½ LEAN MEAT; 1 VEGETABLE; 0 FRUIT; ½ FAT; 0 OTHER CARBOHYDRATES

TASTE TESTER COMMENTS:

"This soup is one of my new favorites and I promise I will make great vats of it during the winter. It's just perfect on a cold day!"
Cost per serving .49

Roasted Vegetable and Lentil Soup

Serves 5

1 (1 to 1 ¼ -pound) eggplant, peeled and diced
4 large plum tomatoes, quartered lengthwise
1 large onion, cut into 8 wedges
½ large green bell pepper, quartered
4 large garlic cloves, peeled
2 tablespoons olive oil

1 cup water (or more if necessary)
2 cans chicken broth
1 ¼ cup dried brown lentils
4 teaspoons cumin
½ cup sour cream

Preheat oven to 450 degrees. In a roasting pan, arrange veggies and garlic and drizzle with olive oil. Roast vegetables for 20 minutes. Give them a stir and roast until tender, stirring occasionally, for another 20 minutes. Remove veggies to a blender, but don't rinse out the roasting pan—just set aside. Blend veggies once cooled a bit. Don't over process—you want them chopped and blended, but not liquefied. Dump this mixture into a large saucepan. On the stove top, add 1 cup water to the roasting pan and heat till boiling, scraping up any browned bits. Add to the large saucepan containing the eggplant mixture. Add remaining water, chicken broth, lentils and cumin and bring to a boil. Reduce heat, cover and simmer until lentils are almost tender, about 30 minutes. Season with salt and pepper to taste and ladle into bowls, garnishing with little blobs of sour cream if desired.

PER SERVING: 330 CALORIES (KCAL); 12G TOTAL FAT; (31% CALORIES FROM FAT); 18G PROTEIN; 41G CARBOHYDRATE; 10MG CHOLESTEROL; 335MG SODIUM FOOD EXCHANGES: 2 GRAIN(STARCH); 1½ LEAN MEAT; 2 VEGETABLE; 0 FRUIT; 2 FAT; 0 OTHER CARBOHYDRATES

Low Country Red Beans and Rice
Serves 8

1 pound red beans, rinsed and cleaned
2 small onions, chopped
1 celery stalk, chopped
1 bell pepper, chopped
2 cloves garlic, pressed
1 cup water
3 cups chicken broth
1 ham hock (or substitute smoked turkey leg)
½ teaspoon dried chili flakes (more if you like more heat)

In your crock pot insert, soak beans overnight (or quick cook them according to package instructions). Drain beans, rinse and place back in the crock pot.   Next, get out a large skillet; heat the oil over medium-high heat. Add celery, onion, bell pepper (Cajun cooks call this the holy trinity) and garlic. Cook until all is softened, about 5 minutes. Transfer this mixture to the crock pot. Now add chicken broth, the ham hock (or smoked turkey leg) and let the mixture cook for 8 to 10 hours. Before serving, chop the meat off the bone, discarding all fat and bone and add the meat back to the bean pot. Then add hot peppers. Serve over hot brown rice with a bottle of Tabasco right on the table. My family prefers salsa and we eat this mess with a little sour cream on the side, too.

PER SERVING: 253 CALORIES (KCAL); 3G TOTAL FAT; (11% CALORIES FROM FAT); 18G PROTEIN; 38G CARBOHYDRATE; 13MG CHOLESTEROL; 314MG SODIUM. FOOD EXCHANGES: 2½ GRAIN(STARCH); 1½ LEAN MEAT; ½ VEGETABLE; 0 FRUIT; 0 FAT; 0 OTHER CARBOHYDRATES

Eeny, Bean-y Chili Bean-y

Serves 4

When you need dinner in a hurry, take out a pot and say this three times over it: "eeny, beany, chili beany." Within minutes you should have dinner ready to go. In the off-chance that fails, try this recipe instead—almost as fast!

1 tablespoon olive oil
4 cloves garlic, pressed
1 small onion, chopped
1 small can diced chilies
1 package taco seasoning or 2
    tablespoons taco seasoning
    mix (see Masterful Mixes,
    page 133, for recipe)
1 (14.5 oz) can diced tomatoes
1 (15 oz) can chicken broth
1 (28 oz.) can pinto beans, drained
1 (15 oz.) can black beans, drained
1 (8 oz.) can corn, drained
salt and pepper to taste

In a skillet, heat oil over medium heat and cook the onion and garlic stirring often till onion is soft. Stir in taco seasoning and continue to cook for about 1 minute. Add the tomatoes with their juice, the beans, corn, broth and salt and pepper to taste. Simmer, stirring occasionally for an hour.

PER SERVING: 171 CALORIES (KCAL); 4G TOTAL FAT; (18% CALORIES FROM FAT); 8G PROTEIN; 29G CARBOHYDRATE; 0MG CHOLESTEROL; 874MG SODIUM. FOOD EXCHANGES: 1 GRAIN (STARCH); ½ LEAN MEAT; 1½ VEGETABLE; 0 FRUIT; ½ FAT; 0 OTHER CARBOHYDRATES

TASTE TESTERS COMMENTS:

"This was so good and so easy! How do you come up with these great recipes? Loved this one. Definitely a keeper."
Cost Per Serving .78

Calypso Beans 'n Rice

Serves 6

1 (15 oz.) can black beans, rinsed, drained (or equivalent of homemade beans)
1 small red onion, sliced thin
2 tablespoons vinegar (if you have balsamic, use that or cider vinegar is fine)
1 tablespoon olive oil
1 onion, chopped
4 large garlic cloves, pressed

1 cup brown rice
2 cans chicken broth (or home-made equivalent)
½ cup dry white wine
2 bay leaves
½ teaspoon curry powder
salt and pepper to taste
pinch of cayenne pepper

Combine the first 3 ingredients in medium bowl. Let stand 30 minutes, stirring occasionally. Season with salt and pepper to taste. While the beans are marinating, heat oil in a saucepan over medium-high heat. Add onion and garlic and sauté until onion is soft, about 3 minutes. Add rice and stir to incorporate. Then add broth, wine, bay leaves, curry powder (now you have something to do with that spice in your cupboard!) and cayenne pepper and blend well. Bring everything to a boil; stirring well. Reduce heat to medium and simmer until rice is tender and mixture is creamy, stirring occasionally, about 20 minutes. Salt and pepper to taste and serve in bowls, cayenne pepper on the side if you're daring.

PER SERVING: 222 CALORIES (KCAL); 2G TOTAL FAT; (8% CALORIES FROM FAT); 8G PROTEIN; 39G CARBOHYDRATE; 0MG CHOLESTEROL; 477MG SODIUM. FOOD EXCHANGES: 2 GRAIN(STARCH); ½ LEAN MEAT; 1 VEGETABLE; 0 FRUIT; 0 FAT; 0 OTHER CARBOHYDRATES

TASTE TESTER COMMENTS:

"Good recipe! Bring on more beans...I love how cheap this was!"
Cost per serving .42

Thanksgiving Soup

Serves 4

Really you don't have to wait until Thanksgiving to enjoy this soup. However, it's a wonderful non-Thanksgiving-y thing to do with leftover turkey that won't taste like leftover turkey. If you have enough leftovers, it might be a good idea to double this and freeze half for another time.

1½ tablespoons olive oil
2 small onions, chopped
1 kielbasa or some other fully cooked sausage you have hanging
    around, sliced in rounds (optional)
2 teaspoons thyme
1 cup dry white wine
3 cans chicken broth
2 (15 oz.) cans Great Northern beans, drained (or homemade
    equivalent)
2½ cups diced leftover turkey leg (or as much as you can get off the
    leg)

Heat oil over medium high heat in a large saucepan. Sauté onion and kielbasa until onion is soft and sausage is light brown, about 5 minutes. Add thyme and wine and simmer until slightly reduced, about 2 minutes. Mix in broth, 1 cup of the beans and the chopped turkey. Mash remaining beans with a fork and add to soup. Simmer for about 10 minutes or so, and season with salt and pepper to taste. If soup seems too thick, add a little water.

PER SERVING: 325 CALORIES (KCAL); 7G TOTAL FAT; (20% CALORIES FROM FAT); 26G PROTEIN; 34G CARBOHYDRATE; 30MG CHOLESTEROL; 425MG SODIUM. FOOD EXCHANGES: 2 GRAIN(STARCH); 2½ LEAN MEAT; ½ VEGETABLE; 0 FRUIT; ½ FAT; 0 OTHER CARBOHYDRATES

(NOTE: fat grams are significantly lowered if you use the new low-fat kielbasa available)

Barbecue Bean Soup

Serves 4

3 onions, chopped
3 garlic cloves, pressed
2 tablespoons olive oil
2 tablespoons chili powder
2 tablespoons cumin
1 teaspoon allspice
2 (32 oz.) cans tomatoes including the juice, chopped
3 (15 oz.) cans of pinto beans, drained and rinsed (or use the
    equivalent in homemade beans)
1 small jar roasted red peppers, rinsed, drained, and chopped
3 cans beef or chicken broth (use equivalent in homemade)
⅓ cup molasses
2 teaspoons cider vinegar, or to taste

In a skillet, heat oil over medium heat and cook the onion and the garlic, stirring often until onion is tender. Stir in chili powder, cumin and allspice and simmer for about a minute. Transfer to a large pot and add the tomatoes with their juice, the beans, roasted peppers, broth, molasses, and salt and pepper to taste. Simmer, stirring occasionally, for about an hour. Stir the vinegar into the soup and simmer the soup until it is heated through.

PER SERVING: 171 CALORIES (KCAL); 4G TOTAL FAT; 8G PROTEIN;
29G CARBOHYDRATES; 0 MG CHOLESTEROL; 847 MG SODIUM.
FOOD EXCHANGES: 1 GRAIN (STARCH); ½ LEAN MEAT; 1½
VEGETABLE; 0 FRUIT; ½ FAT; 0 OTHER CARBOHYDRATES

Tuscany Chicken and Beans

Serves 6

The aroma of this cooking is intoxicating. Keeping the price even lower on this dish is easy if you buy your ingredients in season (the butternut squash) and on sale (the chicken).

6 cups water
1 (15 oz.) can of Great Northern beans (or equivalent of homemade)
1 onion, ½ cut into quarters, the other half chopped
6 chicken thighs
2 tablespoons olive oil
1 tablespoon lemon juice
¾ teaspoon oregano
1 teaspoon thyme
½ teaspoon rosemary
½ cup dry white wine
4 cloves garlic, pressed
1 butternut squash, peeled and diced
1 (15 oz.) can diced tomatoes

Place chicken in a large zipper-type bag. Add 1 tablespoon olive oil, lemon juice, oregano, thyme and rosemary and toss to coat. Let stand for 45 minutes at room temperature, turning the bag often. In the meantime, assemble your other ingredients. Heat remaining olive oil in a skillet over medium high heat. Sprinkle chicken generously with salt and pepper. Cook chicken in the skillet until golden brown, about 4 minutes each side. Put chicken on plate while finishing the recipe. Pour off grease from skillet. Add wine and garlic to skillet, simmering until liquid is reduced by half, scraping up the brown bits with a wire whisk, about 2 minutes. Stir in squash, canned tomatoes and beans. Season with salt and pepper. Add chicken to skillet. Cover and simmer until chicken is cooked through and squash is tender, about 30 to 40 minutes. Then uncover and simmer until sauce thickens slightly, about 3 minutes more. To serve, place chicken on plate and spoon bean mixture over the top.

PER SERVING: 369 CALORIES (KCAL); 8G TOTAL FAT; (18% CALORIES FROM FAT); 23G PROTEIN; 54G CARBOHYDRATE; 57MG CHOLESTEROL; 188MG SODIUM. FOOD EXCHANGES: 3 GRAIN(STARCH); 2½ LEAN MEAT; 1 VEGETABLE; 0 FRUIT; 1 FAT; 0 OTHER CARBOHYDRATES

Baked Bean-ritos

Serves 12

1 onion, chopped
4 garlic cloves, minced
3 tablespoons olive oil
1 (15 oz.) can black beans, drained and rinsed (or use equivalent of homemade beans)
1 (15 oz.) can pinto beans, drained and rinsed (or use equivalent of homemade beans)
1 (15 oz.) can enchilada sauce (try the green enchilada sauce for fun sometime)
½ cup jarred salsa, plus more for serving
3 teaspoons cumin
12 (7- to 8-inch) flour tortillas warmed (I prefer to use whole wheat tortillas)
1½ cups grated Monterey Jack

In a skillet, heat the oil over medium heat and cook the onion and the garlic until the onion is softened, add the beans, and mash about half of them with a potato masher. Add ½ the beans and mash. Then add ½ can of the enchilada sauce, ½ cup salsa, the cumin, and salt and black pepper to taste. Cook on low, simmering the mixture, stirring often, for about 3 minutes. Working with 1 warmed tortilla at a time, keeping the others covered and warm, spread about 3 tablespoons of the filling down the center of each tortilla and roll the tortillas, enclosing the filling but keeping the ends open. Arrange the burritos, seam sides down, in one layer in a baking dish. Add about two tablespoons of water to the remaining half can of enchilada sauce and pour evenly over the top of the burritos (they won't be soaking). Then sprinkle them with the cheese and bake covered with foil in a 350 degree oven for 15 to 20 minutes. Serve the burritos with extra salsa on the side and a nice green salad.

PER SERVING: 428 CALORIES (KCAL); 17G TOTAL FAT; (36% CALORIES FROM FAT); 14G PROTEIN; 54G CARBOHYDRATE; 24MG CHOLESTEROL; 765MG SODIUM. FOOD EXCHANGES: 3½ GRAIN(STARCH); ½ LEAN MEAT; ½ VEGETABLE; 0 FRUIT; 3 FAT; 0 OTHER CARBOHYDRATES

London Fog Split Pea Soup

Serves 8

2 cups split peas, rinsed and picked over
2 tablespoons olive oil
1 onion, chopped
2 carrots, diced
1 teaspoon thyme
1 ham hock (or one smoked turkey leg)
salt and pepper to taste

Put the cleaned split peas in a crock pot. In a skillet, heat the oil over medium heat. Sauté the onion and carrot for about 3 minutes and add to the crock pot. Fill the crock pot with about 10 cups of water and bury the ham hock or smoked turkey leg into the peas. Cook on low for 8 to 10 hours. Serve with crusty bread and a big salad.

PER SERVING: 244 CALORIES (KCAL); 6G TOTAL FAT; (22% CALORIES FROM FAT); 15G PROTEIN; 33G CARBOHYDRATE; 13MG CHOLESTEROL; 22MG SODIUM. FOOD EXCHANGES: 2 GRAIN (STARCH); 1 LEAN MEAT; ½ VEGETABLE; 0 FRUIT; 0 OTHER CARBOHYDRATES

Hoppin' John

Serves 8

This traditional Southern dish is served on New Year's Day for good luck. The black-eyed peas mean good luck and the greens mean money. The best version of Hoppin' John I've ever eaten is Paul Prudhomme's delicious recipe. My version is a lot less fussy than his and pretty darn good in its own right.

1 pound black-eyed peas, soaked overnight, rinsed and drained
1 tablespoon olive oil
2 onions, chopped
1 rib of celery, chopped fine
1 bell pepper, seeded and chopped
2 cloves garlic, pressed
4 cups water
3 cups chicken broth
1 teaspoon crushed pepper
1½ teaspoon thyme
1 teaspoon basil
½ teaspoon marjoram
½ teaspoon oregano
1 pound turkey sausage, cooked and crumbled
salt and pepper to taste
cooked brown rice for serving

In a skillet, heat the oil and add onions, celery and bell pepper. Cook till wilted, stirring often to prevent sticking. Add the garlic, lower heat and cook for another minute. In a crock pot, place the black eyed peas, the cooked veggies from the skillet and add the water, chicken broth, crushed pepper and the rest of seasonings. Cover and cook on low in a crock pot for about 8 hours. Add the cooked sausage, salt and pepper to taste. Serve with bowls of brown rice. Happy New Year, even if you're making this in the middle of October!

PER SERVING: 475 CALORIES (KCAL); 26G TOTAL FAT; (48% CALORIES FROM FAT); 22G PROTEIN; 39G CARBOHYDRATE; 39MG CHOLESTEROL; 683MG SODIUM. FOOD EXCHANGES: 2½ GRAIN(STARCH); 2 LEAN MEAT; ½ VEGETABLE; 0 FRUIT; 4½ FAT; 0 OTHER CARBOHYDRATES

Chapter 5
STEWS, SOUPS AND OTHER CROCK POT TRICKERY

If you're looking for an exercise in futility or want to stretch your capacity for patience, try helping your child clean his room. Or unearth it, as the case may be. Hang on...this really does have something to do with crock pots.

For reasons still unknown by anthropologists, a child's room has always been a place for parental exasperation. Aborigines have been known to make a kid's room reason enough for a tribunal meeting. In the days of the Pilgrims, a mother's voice could clearly be heard at the top of Plymouth Rock, "Clean Thy Room!"

My son's room had reached capacity. It was time to either call the fire marshal and turn him in, or launch a full-scale SWAT team assault on the offending room. No doubt about it, the endless collections of stuff, books, and randomly stashed dirty clothes had taken their toll. Cleaning up the aftermath of Hurricane Hugo looked like child's play compared to this project.

There are certain things in life one should never have to do—like your own biopsy, for example. (Unless of course, you happen to be alone on the frozen tundra at the North Pole just you and your scalpel.) Nonetheless, some things must be done and my son's room was certainly no exception. I took a deep breath and dragged the culprit with me to the scene of the crime.

Standing at the threshold of his room, I stared at 150 square feet of chaos till my eyes began to water. It was as if the Lego™ Fairy had scattered every Lego known to man (or boy) all over the room like fairy dust. The k'Nex™ (another building toy) were no better and though most were made into some sort of weapon, they were laying out all over the floor, as if to dry.

Rocks of every imaginable shape, size and color lined both windowsills. The clean clothes that were supposed to go in the drawers were stacked on the spare bed like leaning Towers of Pisa. And then there was the dust...

But the dust was nothing compared to the Underworld. All moms know about this place, but kids think that somehow under the bed is impervious to a parental probe. Like squirrels hiding provisions for winter, children ferret away quantities of food, dirty clothes and who-knows-what else. It is an instinctual thing to have a bounty for the winter, I suppose. The "stuff" sticking out from under those two beds was evidence enough that there was an entire storehouse of boy paraphernalia I knew I didn't have the capacity to handle. Intuitively, I decided against looking. It was as if a small, still voice whispered in my ear, "Don't go there."

There was still plenty to do. Every two minutes or so I would gasp as I uncovered yet another "treasure". With bulging eyes, I gingerly held up the skin from a big cicada from last summer with one hand and asked, "Why is this here?" as I pointed with the other hand at the open underwear drawer. "I'm saving it," he said. "Oh really?" I replied. "I thought you were fitting it for underwear!"

It was at this point my son's rediscovered missing dress shoes and belt (now three sizes too small) re-emerged, and I realized I couldn't keep this up. It was getting hard to breathe. Suddenly my temples began to throb and I thought I was going to have a stroke. I knew I had to get out of there quick.

Call in the second string. My husband goes upstairs and within minutes, begins threatening a skip loader and blow torch. He'll do anything to wiggle out of hard, manual labor. I was conveniently out of pocket, helping my daughter with the clean up of her room. She's the "neat one" mind you. Or so I thought!

After it was all over and I had fully recovered, I looked back with perfect hindsight. Should you take on a project of this proportion during your weekend, let me make a one-word suggestion for dinner:

Crock-pot.

And here is the perfect place to start. A crock-pot recipe I wished I had made, that day of days. It's a good one in time of emergency or excavation.

Mama's Chicken Stew

Serves 10

1 pound skinned, boneless chicken breasts, cut into bite-size pieces
1 pound skinned, boneless chicken thighs, cut into bite-size pieces
½ cup water
1 cup frozen small onions
½ cup celery, sliced
2 cups frozen petite green peas

1 cup carrots, sliced thin
1 teaspoon paprika
½ teaspoon sage
½ thyme
2 teaspoons garlic powder
salt and pepper to taste
2 (14.5 oz.) cans chicken broth
1 (6 oz.) can tomato paste
¼ cup water
3 tablespoons cornstarch

Combine first 14 ingredients (except the peas) in a crock-pot. Cover with lid, and cook on the high-heat setting for 4 hours or until carrots are fork tender. Combine water and cornstarch in a small bowl, stirring with a wire whisk until blended—no lumps allowed. Add cornstarch mixture and peas to slow cooker; stir well. Cover and cook on the high-heat setting for an additional 30 minutes. Correct the seasoning if necessary and serve over a big scoop of mashed potatoes.

PER SERVING: 154 CALORIES (KCAL); 2G TOTAL FAT; (13% CALORIES FROM FAT); 20G PROTEIN; 13G CARBOHYDRATE; 48MG CHOLESTEROL; 492MG SODIUM. FOOD EXCHANGES: ½ GRAIN (STARCH); 2½ LEAN MEAT; 1 VEGETABLE; 0 FRUIT; 0 FAT; 0 OTHER CARBOHYDRATES

TASTE TESTER COMMENTS:

"This was as easy as it was delicious. You could easily serve this to company. I served it over pasta which was good, but I think it would have been better with rice, so you could get more gravy with each bite. Even my youngest, who really dislikes veggies ate it up! "
Cost per serving .77

Your Basic Beef Stew

Serves 6

1½ pound stew beef cut up, sprinkled with 1 tablespoon (or so) of flour
2 tablespoons olive oil
1 medium onion, chopped
1½ cups water, wine or beer (I make mine with water)
3 carrots peeled and chopped
½ tablespoon of thyme
½ tablespoon of garlic
salt and pepper to taste

In a Dutch oven, heat your oil and add the onion and carrot. Sauté for a minute or two and add the beef. Let the beef cook for a few minutes, stirring occasionally till browned. Then pour beef mixture into a crock pot. Take 1 ½ cups of water, wine or beer (depending on the flavor you want) and pour into the Dutch oven and turn on high (if you do use wine or beer, add ½ cup of water). Using a spatula, get all the browned bits up and let it boil for approximately 10 minutes. Reduce to simmer and continue cooking till meat is tender (approx. 4 hours) before serving. Serve with mashed potatoes or buttered noodles or rice.

PER SERVING: 410 CALORIES (KCAL); 28G TOTAL FAT; (62% CALORIES FROM FAT); 32G PROTEIN; 6G CARBOHYDRATE; 113MG CHOLESTEROL; 348MG SODIUM. FOOD EXCHANGES: 0 GRAIN (STARCH); 4½ LEAN MEAT; 1 VEGETABLE; 0 FRUIT; 2½ FAT; 0 OTHER CARBOHYDRATES

TASTE TESTER COMMENTS:

"Not only VERY good, but also very versatile recipe, and reheats well. For a smaller family, this is a winner. I also see all kinds of possibilities alternating vegetables, and exchanging noodles for mashed potatoes. Cost can't be beat if several items are on sale."
Cost per serving .98

Tex-Mex Chili

Serves 6

¾ pound ground beef (extra lean will keep the fat grams lower)
1 can (15 oz.) pinto beans
1 large onion, chopped
2 large cloves garlic, pressed
1 (14.5 oz.) can diced tomatoes
1 (7 oz.) can diced green chilies, drained
1 (8.5 oz.) can whole-kernel corn, un-drained
1½ teaspoons oregano
2 teaspoons cumin
salt and pepper to taste
¼ teaspoon cayenne pepper (optional)
2 tablespoons masa (corn flour –found in the ethnic section of the
  grocery store, used for making tortillas)

Brown beef, drain off fat and place in crock-pot. Next, add the rest of the ingredients, except the masa flour and stir to combine. Cover and cook on low for about 5 hours. Then, turn control to high. While waiting for the crock-pot to heat up, stir ½ cup of cold water into the 2 tablespoons of masa and mix well with a fork till fully incorporated. Add to crock-pot mixture and allow to heat for another hour or so. At this point, you can't kill it! Serve in bowls with shredded cheese on top, if desired.

PER SERVING: 259 CALORIES (KCAL); 11G TOTAL FAT; (36% CALORIES FROM FAT); 16G PROTEIN; 26G CARBOHYDRATE; 39MG CHOLESTEROL; 428MG SODIUM. FOOD EXCHANGES: 1 GRAIN(STARCH); 1½ LEAN MEAT; 1½ VEGETABLE; 0 FRUIT; 1 FAT; 0 OTHER CARBOHYDRATES

TASTE TESTER COMMENTS:

"A great Chili meal for a chilly day! Everyone loved this—super easy, yummy and very economical! We added corn muffins and cole slaw for a complete relaxing meal!"
Cost per serving: $0.68

Corny Chicken and Potato Chowder

Serves 4

1 tablespoon olive oil
6 slices turkey bacon, chopped (optional)
2 medium onions, chopped
2 cans chicken broth
2 good sized potatoes, peeled, cut into ½ inch pieces
4 cups corn kernels, frozen or canned (either two cans or two
  packages of frozen)
2 cups cooked chicken, chopped
1½ teaspoons thyme
1 cup milk
salt and pepper to taste

Cook bacon with olive oil in a large saucepan over medium-high heat until brown and crisp, about 5 minutes. Remove bacon to paper towels and drain, setting aside for later. Add onion, sautéing until soft, about 3 minutes. Place soft onions into the crock pot. Add broth to the skillet, turning the heat up and with a wire whisk get all the browned bits from the sauce pan. Pour broth into the crock pot as well and add potatoes. Cover and let cook on low for 8 hours. Turn crock pot heat to high and add corn, chicken, thyme and milk. Cover and allow to cook for another hour. Season chowder to taste with salt and pepper. Ladle into bowls. Crumble bacon over the top and serve.

PER SERVING: 274 CALORIES (KCAL); 9G TOTAL FAT; (30% CALORIES FROM FAT); 22G PROTEIN; 26G CARBOHYDRATE; 58MG CHOLESTEROL; 680MG SODIUM. FOOD EXCHANGES: 1½ GRAIN(STARCH); 2½ LEAN MEAT; ½ VEGETABLE; 0 FRUIT; 1 FAT; 0 OTHER CARBOHYDRATES

Chinese Crockpot Chicken

Serves 8

This is wonderfully easy and cheap! The recipe originally called for a pork roast, but that's too pricey (and greasy) and the chicken turned out fragrant and wonderful. This is a keeper!

1 whole chicken (about 3 pounds)
¼ cup soy sauce
¼ cup orange marmalade
2 tablespoons ketchup
6 cloves garlic, pressed
1 onion, sliced
Salt and pepper to taste

Place your chicken in the crock-pot. Mix together soy sauce, marmalade and ketchup and pour over the top of the chicken. Then add garlic and onions, a teeny bit of salt (won't need much because of the soy sauce) and pepper. Put the lid on the crock-pot and cook on low for about 10 to 12 hours. Chicken should be falling off the bone when ready. Serve it with rice, veggies and the sauce on the side.

PER SERVING: 444 CALORIES (KCAL); 29G TOTAL FAT; (60% CALORIES FROM FAT); 33G PROTEIN; 11G CARBOHYDRATE; 170MG CHOLESTEROL; 481MG SODIUM. FOOD EXCHANGES: 0 GRAIN(STARCH); 4½ LEAN MEAT; ½ VEGETABLE; 0 FRUIT; 3 FAT; ½ OTHER CARBOHYDRATES

TASTE TESTER COMMENTS:
"Easy and delicious! My whole family loved this."
Cost per serving .79

Pot Roast 1, 2, 3

This pot roast recipe takes your pot roast to new places. Like the famous Rubber Chicken recipe, this recipe recycles your pot roast into three recipes. So instead of having leftovers, you can sneak in two more entrees without anyone being the wiser. The secret to pulling this off is lots of vegetables served with this delicious pot roast.

POT ROAST 1
No Frills Crock Pot Roast
Serves 12 – Or 4 Each Meal

1 tablespoon olive oil
1 (3 to 4) pound pot roast, left
   whole
salt and pepper to taste
2 teaspoons thyme

1 medium onion, sliced
1 carrot, sliced
6 potatoes, sliced
1 bay leaf
½ cup water

In a large skillet, heat the oil and brown the beef on all sides. Put the roast in the crock-pot and liberally season with salt and pepper. In the same skillet, sauté the onions, carrots and potatoes for about 3 minutes. Pour the veggies on top of the beef. Return the skillet one more time to the stovetop and heat the water in the skillet, using a wire whisk to get up all the browned bits from the bottom of the pan. Pour this warmed water over the top of your beef. Add the bay leaf and cook on low for 8 to 10 hours. Remove beef and let it rest for about 10 minutes before slicing. Remove veggies and put in a serving dish. If you want, you can make a thickened gravy with the cooking juices, or just serve as is. I usually serve baked sweet potatoes and steamed green beans with the rest of the cooked vegetables to extend the life of the roast, so to speak, but use what you have. Petite peas would be good, too.

PER SERVING: 301 CALORIES (KCAL); 19G TOTAL FAT; (57% CALORIES FROM FAT); 19G PROTEIN; 13G CARBOHYDRATE; 66MG CHOLESTEROL; 63MG SODIUM. FOOD EXCHANGES: ½ GRAIN(STARCH); 2½ LEAN MEAT; ½ VEGETABLE; 0 FRUIT; 2 FAT; 0 OTHER CARBOHYDRATES

POT ROAST 2
Shredded Beefwiches

With any luck, you have quite a bit of beef left (let's assume about 2 pounds). Shred the beef with two forks, and heat on the stove top. Serve on crusty rolls with a little cheese and sautéed onions and some sauce for dipping. We like horseradish on ours. A large salad would go perfect with this sandwich supper. If you can, stretch this beef to just one more meal—it's a good one!

POT ROAST 3
Soft Tacos

Take the remaining shredded beef out of the refrigerator and throw it in a saucepan with 3 tablespoons of Mexican seasoning and add a little water. Let cook on low for about 15 minutes. In the meantime, fix your fixin's. Shred lettuce, chop tomato, chop some cilantro if you like...whatever stuff you have around. Serve wrapped in warmed corn tortillas with shredded lettuce, cheese, salsa and hefty sides of brown rice and black beans.

PER SERVING: 40 CALORIES (KCAL); 3G TOTAL FAT; (60% CALORIES FROM FAT); 1G PROTEIN; 4G CARBOHYDRATE; 0MG CHOLESTEROL; 5MG SODIUM. FOOD EXCHANGES: 0 GRAIN(STARCH); 0 LEAN MEAT; ½ VEGETABLE; 0 FRUIT; ½ FAT; 0 OTHER CARBOHYDRATES

Italiano Beef Stew

Serves 4

1 pound lean beef, round steak would work
1 (14½-oz.) can stewed tomatoes
2 tablespoons dry red wine, optional
2 teaspoons Italian seasoning, crushed
2 teaspoons garlic powder
2 tablespoons olive oil
⅓ teaspoon ground red pepper
3 medium carrots, cut in thin slices
3 small turnips, cut in ½" slices, optional
1 large onion, chopped
1 (9 oz.) bag Italian (or pole) green beans, frozen

In a Dutch oven over medium-high heat, brown beef and season with salt and pepper. Put beef mixture in a crock-pot and add next 8 ingredients, let cook on low for 5 to 6 hours. Increase the heat to high and add wine and green beans and cook till beans are tender. You could serve this with pasta, but I like it with good old-fashioned mashed potatoes.

PER SERVING: 364 CALORIES (KCAL); 15G TOTAL FAT; (37% CALORIES FROM FAT); 32G PROTEIN; 25G CARBOHYDRATE; 54MG CHOLESTEROL; 1454MG SODIUM

TASTE TESTER COMMENTS:

"Yum! This dish made the house smell so good! We all thought it was delicious. Serve this when you don't want to be bothered with leftovers, there won't be any! We had with mashed potatoes but would have been delicious with pasta. The green beans added a lot to this dish."

Cost per Serving .89

Barbecue-in-a-Pot Beef

Serves 9

This wonderful recipe couldn't get any easier. Make sure you use a lean cut of beef and enjoy the tasty sandwiches.

**1 (3) pound round roast, chuck roast
   or whatever else you found on sale
1½ cup barbecue sauce
8 hamburger buns, sliced open**

Heat the oil in your skillet and brown your beef. Salt and pepper it liberally and place it in the crock-pot. Cook on low for 8 to 10 hours. Remove from crock pot and let rest about 10 minutes. Either slice thinly or shred with forks and place open faced on a hamburger bun. Reserve sauce from cooking (you may need to skim some of the fat off the top) and use for dipping. Delicious served with coleslaw or a salad.

PER SERVING: 349 CALORIES (KCAL); 10G TOTAL FAT; (26% CALORIES FROM FAT); 37G PROTEIN; 25G CARBOHYDRATE; 88MG CHOLESTEROL; 640MG SODIUM. FOOD EXCHANGES: 1½ GRAIN(STARCH); 4½ LEAN MEAT; 0 VEGETABLE; 0 FRUIT; ½ FAT; ½ OTHER CARBOHYDRATES

South African Chicken

Serves 6

This completely delicious chicken dish comes from Africa. Yassa, is the national dish of Senegal and is served traditionally over white rice. I changed that to brown rice and love broccoli served on the side with this one. It needs to be marinated overnight, so start this recipe when you're cleaning up dinner dishes the night before.

6 onions, sliced thin
6 cloves of garlic, pressed
¼ cup lemon juice
salt and pepper to taste
1 (3 to 4) pound chicken cut up (see How to Chicken Dissection 101 on
**   page 46)**
1 tablespoon olive oil

In a large zipper-type bag, combine onions, garlic, lemon juice, salt and pepper. Add chicken and zip up the bag. Roll the chicken around in the bag to coat. Refrigerate overnight, turning the chicken if you get a chance.   Remove chicken from the marinade and put marinade in the crock-pot. In a skillet, heat oil over medium high heat and add the chicken. When the chicken is browned, put dark meat pieces in crock pot first, finally adding the breast portions on top. Cook on low for 4 to 6 hours, depending on your crock pot. When done, remove chicken and transfer remaining cooking juices and onions to skillet. Cook the onions and liquid for about 10 minutes until reduced to half. Serve chicken with brown rice and spoon the sauce generously over everything.

PER SERVING: 453 CALORIES (KCAL); 31G TOTAL FAT; (62% CALORIES FROM FAT); 33G PROTEIN; 9G CARBOHYDRATE; 170MG CHOLESTEROL; 133MG SODIUM. FOOD EXCHANGES: 0 GRAIN(STARCH); 4½ LEAN MEAT; 1½ VEGETABLE; 0 FRUIT; 3½ FAT; 0 OTHER CARBOHYDRATES

Chapter 6
GOING MEATLESS

Children can be difficult.
If you're a parent, you know THIS is the understatement of the century. They are small humans with big wills, all their own. The strong-willed child, that creature we've all heard about from the popular child experts and their cronies, lives at almost everyone's house, wreaking havoc at the dinner table. Or so I hear. Of course, being a nutritionist and former caterer, I have never had to dip my toe in that pool. My children eat perfectly. And if you believe that, can I interest you in an ocean front time share in Iceland?

I have also noticed that certain things your parents may have said come back to haunt you as you spew them from your own mouth. My very favorite is, "Eat it, it's good for you." Did I really say that? The echo from those words sounded almost exactly like my mother. And I meant it—that's the scary part. It's that moment in parenting that we begin to feel schizophrenic. We say things we mean, yet hate hearing our own voices say them. Or worse, we hear our OWN parents saying them as our mouths open and pronounce the syllables. It's a frightening experience—fraught with I and angst-ridden flashbacks.

Once the words, "eat it, it's good for you" actually do leave your mouth, you know what's coming next. You can almost hear your child's eyes rolling around in their sockets and suddenly feel incredibly stupid for saying it in the first place. What were you expecting? "Oh gosh Mom, why didn't you tell me it's good for me? NOW I'll eat it!" As if...

That is why it's important to lie to your children about what their food contains. Don't you dare tell them the lasagna they just scarfed down had tofu in it and don't even try explaining TVP. Some food secrets you'll just have to take to your grave.

Hot Tamale Lentil Casserole

Serves 8

1 tablespoon olive oil
1 large onion, chopped
1 small bell pepper, chopped
2 cloves garlic, pressed
3 cups water
1¼ cup dried lentils, sorted and rinsed
1 (14 oz.) can tomatoes, diced, with juice
1 package taco seasoning mix (or equivalent homemade, see
    Masterful Mixes, page 133)

CHEESE CORNBREAD TOPPING:
½ cup shredded Cheddar cheese
¼ cup milk
1 (8.5 oz.) package cornbread muffin mix
1 (8.5 oz.) can cream-style corn
1 large egg

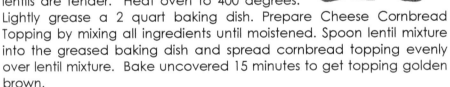

Heat olive oil in a 3 quart saucepan over a medium-high heat. Cook onion, bell pepper and garlic in oil, stirring frequently, until vegetables are crisp tender. Stir in water, lentils, diced tomatoes with juice and seasoning mix; reduce heat to low. Partially cover and simmer 35 to 40 minutes or until lentils are tender. Heat oven to 400 degrees. Lightly grease a 2 quart baking dish. Prepare Cheese Cornbread Topping by mixing all ingredients until moistened. Spoon lentil mixture into the greased baking dish and spread cornbread topping evenly over lentil mixture. Bake uncovered 15 minutes to get topping golden brown.

PER SERVING: 770 CALORIES (KCAL); 18G TOTAL FAT; (21% CALORIES FROM FAT); 23G PROTEIN; 133G CARBOHYDRATE; 27MG CHOLESTEROL; 2074MG SODIUM. FOOD EXCHANGES: 3 GRAIN(STARCH); 1 LEAN MEAT; 1 VEGETABLE; 0 FRUIT; 3½ FAT; 6 OTHER CARBOHYDRATES

TASTE TESTER COMMENTS:

"Ole! A very filling and satisfying (vegetarian!) dish. Our 12 year old resident meat and potatoes guy said, 'I like it. This is good. This is good!'"
Cost per serving: .56 (milk, oil & seasoning on hand)

Spinach Noodle Casserole

Serves 8

8 ounces egg noodles
3 tablespoons butter
2 tablespoons flour
1 cup milk
½ teaspoon paprika
salt and pepper to taste
⅓ teaspoon nutmeg
2 (10 oz.) packages frozen spinach, cooked and drained
½ pound Swiss cheese – shredded

Cook noodles according to package directions until just tender; drain and rinse. In saucepan, melt butter; stir in flour and cook, stirring, one minute. Gradually add milk and bring to a boil. Cook until thick, stirring constantly. Add seasonings and spinach. Stir and remove from heat. In greased baking dish, arrange half of the noodles, and sprinkle with half of the cheese; spoon spinach mixture over cheese. Add another layer of noodles and sprinkle with remaining cheese. Cover, and bake at 400 degrees for 15 minutes. Remove cover and bake 15 minutes more.

PER SERVING: 296 CALORIES (KCAL); 15G TOTAL FAT; (43% CALORIES FROM FAT); 15G PROTEIN; 27G CARBOHYDRATE; 69MG CHOLESTEROL; 324MG SODIUM

TASTE TESTER COMMENTS:

"This is a time saving meal, a big plus around this busy home! It was a hit with the adults, less so with children but they did fairly well considering it was spinach! The flavors blend so well together and it was much lighter than your typical sauced casserole. Popeye would be proud."

Frannie's Tomato Pie

Serves 8

One deep-dish pie shell, pierced
¼ cup Parmesan cheese (I prefer Romano—but this is Frannie's recipe)
2 medium ripe tomatoes, peeled and thinly sliced
1 medium onion, thinly sliced
½ teaspoon basil
½ teaspoon Italian seasoning
2 teaspoons olive oil
½ cup mayonnaise
1 cup cheddar cheese

Partially cook pie crust in 400 degree oven, until lightly browned, about 10 minutes. Meanwhile, mix mayonnaise and cheddar cheese together. Set aside. Sprinkle Parmesan cheese on the bottom of the crust. Layer tomatoes and onions, then season with salt, pepper, Italian seasoning and basil to taste. Repeat layers. Drizzle olive oil on 2nd layer. Top with mayonnaise and cheese mixture. Bake at 350 degrees for 40 minutes, reduce heat to 200 for 10-15 more minutes. Cut in wedges and serve with a fruit salad and muffins.

PER SERVING: 173 CALORIES (KCAL); 10G TOTAL FAT; (50% CALORIES FROM FAT); 7G PROTEIN; 15G CARBOHYDRATE; 11MG CHOLESTEROL; 358MG SODIUM. FOOD EXCHANGES: ½ GRAIN(STARCH); ½ LEAN MEAT; ½ VEGETABLE; 0 FRUIT; 1½ FAT; 0 OTHER CARBOHYDRATES

Angry Crock Sauce

Makes Approximately 5 Cups

This is actually my version of Arrabbiata sauce. Arrabbiata means angry in Italian—bet you didn't know that! Here's a great recipe to use up all those wonderful tomatoes available in the summer. Whether you grow them yourself, have a friendly gardener-type give them to you, or buy them at the height of the season by the bushel at a roadside stand, you don't want to miss making several batches of this flavorful sauce. It's easy and delicious and will pinch hit for you in any lasagna or spaghetti recipe with ease.

1   pound plum tomatoes, cut into ½-inch pieces
1   fresh hot chili, ribbed and seeded and finely chopped (use a Serrano, jalapeno—whatever)
2   tablespoons olive oil
4   large garlic cloves, finely chopped
3   tablespoons dried basil or ½ cup fresh basil leaves, if you have them

In a crock pot, add all ingredients and cook on low all day—about 8 to 10 hours. Let the sauce cool and either make something with it right then, or freeze in freezer-type zipper bags, making sure you label and date.

PER SERVING: 40 CALORIES (KCAL); 3G TOTAL FAT; (60% CALORIES FROM FAT); 1G PROTEIN; 4G CARBOHYDRATE; 0MG CHOLESTEROL; 5MG SODIUM. FOOD EXCHANGES: 0 GRAIN(STARCH); 0 LEAN MEAT; ½ VEGETABLE; 0 FRUIT; ½ FAT; 0 OTHER CARBOHYDRATES

Cheesy Eggplant-Orzo Casserole
Serves 8

2 tablespoons sun-dried tomatoes
½ cup boiling water
1 tablespoon olive oil
6 cups diced peeled eggplant (about 1 ¼ pounds)
1 large onion, diced
1 cup red bell pepper, chopped
1 clove garlic, pressed
salt and pepper to taste
1 cup diced tomato
3 cups cooked orzo (about 1 ½ cups
    uncooked rice-shaped pasta)
1 ½ cups Ricotta cheese (fat-free)
1 cup tomato juice
½ cup fresh basil, chopped
1 (8oz.) can tomato sauce
1 cup dry bread crumbs
½ cup grated Romano cheese, divided

Preheat oven to 350 degrees. Combine sun-dried tomatoes and boiling water in a small bowl; cover and let stand 10 minutes or until soft. Drain, and set aside. Heat oil in a large nonstick skillet over medium-high heat. Add eggplant, onion, bell pepper, and garlic; sauté 5 minutes. Add diced tomato; cook 2 minutes. Add sun-dried tomatoes, orzo, and next 4 ingredients (orzo through tomato sauce,) then add ¼ cup of the Romano cheese and stir well. Spoon orzo mixture into a 13 × 9-inch baking dish. Combine breadcrumbs and remaining cheese; sprinkle crumb topping over orzo mixture. Cover and bake at 350 degrees for 30 minutes or until thoroughly heated. Uncover and bake an additional 10 minutes or until lightly browned.

PER SERVING: 298 CALORIES (KCAL); 8G TOTAL FAT; (23% CALORIES FROM FAT); 16G PROTEIN; 42G CARBOHYDRATE; 11MG CHOLESTEROL; 445MG SODIUM

TASTE TESTER COMMENTS:
"Absolutely delicious – a great combination of unusual ingredients. Eat is not missed a bit! Orzo was new for us – a fun textured pasta! Must admit I am not a fan of most fat free products but fat free ricotta did not give up an inch of flavor."

Four-Cheese Vegetable Lasagna

Serves 9

12 uncooked lasagna noodles
2 teaspoons olive oil
non-aerosol cooking spray (see notes page 15)
2 cups broccoli, chopped
1½ cups carrots, thinly sliced
1 cup green onions, thinly sliced
½ cup red bell pepper, chopped
3 cloves garlic, pressed
½ cup flour
3 cups milk

½ cup grated fresh Romano cheese, divided
salt and pepper to taste
1 (10 oz.) package frozen chopped spinach, thawed, drained, and squeezed dry
1½ cups low-fat cottage cheese
1 cup shredded part-skim Mozzarella cheese
½ cup shredded Swiss cheese
fresh ground pepper

Preheat oven to 375 degrees. Heat oil in a Dutch oven coated with cooking spray over medium heat until hot. Add broccoli and next 4 ingredients (broccoli through garlic), and sauté for approximately 5 minutes. Set aside. To make a white sauce, place flour in a medium saucepan and slowly add milk, stirring with a whisk until blended. Bring to a boil over medium heat; cook 3-5 minutes or until thickened, stirring constantly. Add ¼ cup Romano cheese, salt and pepper. Continue cooking about a minute longer, stirring constantly. Remove from heat; stir in spinach. Combine cheeses well. Spread ½ cup spinach mixture in the bottom of a lightly greased, 13 x 9 inch baking dish. Arrange 4 lasagna noodles on top of the spinach mixture and alternate with cottage cheese mixture, broccoli mixture, and spinach mixture, repeating the layers till you end with noodles. Pour ¾ cup of water over the top and tent tightly with foil. Cover and bake at 375 degrees for an hour or till lasagna noodles are tender. When finished baking, remove foil and top with reserved Romano cheese. Let stand 10 minutes before cutting.

PER SERVING: 583 CALORIES (KCAL); 4G TOTAL FAT; (5% CALORIES FROM FAT); 32G PROTEIN; 104G CARBOHYDRATE; 12MG CHOLESTEROL; 530MG SODIUM

Summer Vegetarian Lasagna

Serves 4

1 onion, chopped
1 large eggplant, peeled and diced
1 squash, any kind, chopped
1 package of tofu, drained and whirled in the blender with parsley and garlic
2 cans of spaghetti sauce
1 cup mozzarella
¼ cup Romano cheese
1 package lasagna noodles, uncooked

In a skillet, heat olive oil and sauté onion and eggplant until soft, about 6 minutes. Remove from the pan and set aside. Add more olive oil and sauté the squash, seasoning with salt and pepper. On the bottom of a small, non-metal, rectangular baking dish, pour about ½ cup of spaghetti sauce and even out. Then layer lasagna noodles, as usual. Next, eggplant, then more sauce, then tofu, then noodles, then squash, then tofu, then sauce, then noodles and finish it off with whatever you have. Make a tent with foil (you don't want it touching your creation or you'll have a chemical reaction with the foil and the tomato) and bake at 350 for 40 minutes (give or take—it will depend on your noodles). When it's done top with grated mozzarella and Romano (or whatever you have on hand) and bake for an additional 10 minutes without the foil.

PER SERVING: 294 CALORIES (KCAL); 12G TOTAL FAT; (34% CALORIES FROM FAT); 16G PROTEIN; 34G CARBOHYDRATE; 15MG CHOLESTEROL; 578MG SODIUM. FOOD EXCHANGES: ½ GRAIN(STARCH); 2 LEAN MEAT; 4 VEGETABLE; 0 FRUIT; 1½ FAT; 0 OTHER CARBOHYDRATES

Vegedillas

Serves 4

1 zucchini, grated
1 yellow squash, grated (you want enough veggies to make at least a
  cup)
1 cup cheddar cheese, grated
16 corn tortillas
A little olive oil

In a bowl, toss the grated zucchini, yellow squash and cheese. Heat a griddle on medium heat and add a little olive oil. Put down as many tortillas as the griddle will handle, after they have warmed for about two minutes, put a little cheese/veggie mixture on each tortilla. Let them cook for another minute or two and then smash them together to make a sandwich. Let the vegedillas cool before cutting them in fourths. Serve with lots of salsa.

PER SERVING: 349 CALORIES (KCAL); 12G TOTAL FAT; (29% CALORIES FROM
FAT); 14G PROTEIN; 50G CARBOHYDRATE; 30MG CHOLESTEROL; 339MG SODIUM. FOOD EXCHANGES: 3
GRAIN(STARCH); 1 LEAN MEAT; ½ VEGETABLE; 0 FRUIT; 1½ FAT; 0 OTHER CARBOHYDRATES

Noodle Eggplant Casserole

Serves 4

8 ounces egg noodles
1 eggplant, peeled and cut into ¼-inch slices
4 egg whites
¾ cup fine dry bread crumbs
1 (16 oz.) can tomato sauce
½ teaspoon garlic powder
⅛ teaspoon pepper
½ teaspoon oregano
⅓ cup grated Parmesan cheese, divided
½ cup Mozzarella cheese, thinly sliced, divided

Prepare noodles according to package directions. While noodles are cooking, dip each slice of eggplant into egg white, then into bread crumbs. Coat each side well. Spray a cookie sheet with non-aerosol vegetable cooking spray. Place eggplant slices on cookie sheet and place under broiler for 3 to 4 minutes on each side, or until lightly browned. Preheat oven to 375 degrees. In a medium bowl, combine tomatoes, tomato sauce, garlic powder, pepper and oregano. When noodles are done, drain well. Spray a 2-quart baking dish with cooking spray. Place a layer of eggplant in bottom of baking dish. Layer half the noodles, followed by half the tomato mixture. Sprinkle half the Parmesan cheese and half the Mozzarella cheese on top. Repeat the layers. Cover with foil and bake for 30 minutes. Remove foil and continue baking 15 minutes, until cheese is melted and top is lightly browned.

PER SERVING: 519 CALORIES (KCAL); 14G TOTAL FAT; (24% CALORIES FROM FAT); 27G PROTEIN; 73G CARBOHYDRATE; 75MG CHOLESTEROL; 1210MG SODIUM

TASTE TESTER COMMENTS:

"A better name for this one might be, Elegant Italian Eggplant Casserole. Although my kids aren't eggplant fans, the combined flavors in this recipe really work!"
Cost per serving: $0.97
(I really think this is more than four servings, though!)

Chapter 7
THE EGG & I

Long, long ago on a farm far, far away, lived a suburban family with a feed store bill that was able to bring tears to a grown man's eyes. With two cows, four goats, umpteen chickens, rabbits, dogs and cats, the feed store people squealed with delight when the mom pulled up in her station wagon and lifted up the back latch before even setting foot into the store.

That mom was me. I was an urban drop-out, eagerly looking for the Simple Life. Tranquil, pastoral, uncomplicated.

What I got was endless chores, feed bills and the heartbreak of a backed up septic tank.

I'll never forget hatching out our first chickens and then watching the dogs eat them one by one. The joy of the first egg and then wondering what to do with 30 eggs a day. I still smile when I remember my daughter running down the hill with the goats leaping behind her, singing at the top of her lungs, "The hills are alive...."

And the garden! Honestly, mine looked like it belonged on the cover of Organic Gardening. I had everything growing and then some. I mulched, fertilized and composted my way to a mighty bounty. I was someone you avoided at church in case I had a squash hiding behind me for you to take home. You know the types—they're the ones with zucchini on their desks at work the size of a small aircraft carrier.

And after the animals were tended, the garden weeded, watered and harvested, there was canning to do. Jams to make. Pickles to pack. Did I mention there was also no air conditioning?

You haven't lived until you have heard me moan about the heat. I just don't do well in this Southern, humidifying oven of a climate in August. It is to me, *unthinkable* to even **think** about setting foot outside in such abominable conditions. Happiness to me is central air set on Polar. Forget being frugal. This is one area where my very sanity is at stake. You and I both know the electric power people like to send those little flyers with your bill trying to make you feel guilty for being comfortable. Do they really think we're that stupid and will reset our thermostats to 85 because they spent money on a flyer?

Last summer, when my daughter sprained her ankle, I asked her if she could wait till fall to go to the ER. Did I mention that I just don't do well in the heat? My family was thinking they would pack me in dry ice on Memorial Day and let me out after Labor Day. That would be fine with me. I won't even tell you what I felt like after canning 24 quarts of pickles, 36 jars of jam and 21 jars of okra. Road kill doesn't talk.

So did I learn any lessons? Not really. After a stint of big city livin', we're back in the country with more animals (added ducks this time), the same ol' station wagon with feed perpetually in the back, but this time we have central air. A big'un. 4 tons of cold power, able to refrigerate the entire South. And that, my dear friends, is living! I might even attempt to can again—maybe.

But in the meantime, I have eggs—lots of them. And even if I didn't have my own personal egg stash, I know I would put eggs on my grocery list every week.

NUTRITION AND EGGS

There was an ad campaign years ago, declaring eggs to be "incredible and edible." Eggs have been given the nutritional shaft for a long time because of the cholesterol factor, but at long last, even the so-called "experts" are now declaring eggs to be the nutritional giants they have always been.

In any case, while eggs pack a strong nutritional punch, they're also cheap. Consider this: a dozen eggs can be had for easily under $2, and a lot of times are just over $1. A high quality, protein rich food—and cheap. All you need are some great recipes to give this versatile pre-chicken a place on your dinner menu.

For starters, how about having Breakfast for Dinner? Kids will especially love it if you serve their scrambled eggs on your good china with orange juice in wine glasses. You could even throw in some candlelight and music—who says cheap needs to be boring? And breakfast for dinner is about as perfect as you can get if you're a *frantic family.*

Cheese Strata

Serves 6

⅓ cup butter, softened
½ teaspoon dry mustard
1 clove garlic, pressed
10 slices old bread (French is good)
2 cups shredded extra sharp cheddar cheese
2 tablespoons parsley, chopped
2 tablespoons onion, chopped
salt and pepper to taste
½ teaspoon Worcestershire sauce
dash of cayenne pepper
4 eggs
2½ cups milk

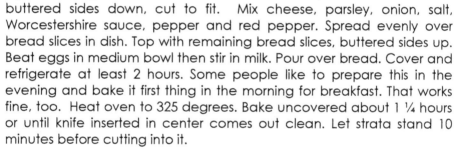

Mix butter, mustard and garlic. Spread evenly over each slice of bread. Cut each slice into thirds. Line bottom and sides of un-greased 8 x 8 square baking dish with half of the bread slices, buttered sides down, cut to fit. Mix cheese, parsley, onion, salt, Worcestershire sauce, pepper and red pepper. Spread evenly over bread slices in dish. Top with remaining bread slices, buttered sides up. Beat eggs in medium bowl then stir in milk. Pour over bread. Cover and refrigerate at least 2 hours. Some people like to prepare this in the evening and bake it first thing in the morning for breakfast. That works fine, too. Heat oven to 325 degrees. Bake uncovered about 1 ¼ hours or until knife inserted in center comes out clean. Let strata stand 10 minutes before cutting into it.

PER SERVING: 289 CALORIES (KCAL); 16G TOTAL FAT; (48% CALORIES FROM FAT); 11G PROTEIN; 26G CARBOHYDRATE; 160MG CHOLESTEROL; 394MG SODIUM. FOOD EXCHANGES: 1½ GRAIN(STARCH); ½ LEAN MEAT; 0 VEGETABLE; 0 FRUIT; 3 FAT; 0 OTHER CARBOHYDRATES

Veggie & Cheese Strata

Serves 4

8 slices old bread
¾ cup Swiss cheese, shredded
2 green onions, minced
3 eggs, slightly beaten
1¼ cups milk
¼ cup mayonnaise
½ teaspoon Tabasco
½ teaspoon basil
dash salt
1 tomato, sliced
3 roasted bell pepper strips (come in a jar, optional)

Use a 9 X 9-inch pan or baking dish. Grease the pan with margarine. Place 4 slices of the bread in the bottom of pan. Sprinkle with ½ cup of the cheese and the green onions. Top with remaining bread slices. Combine eggs, milk, mayonnaise, Tabasco, basil and salt in small bowl; mix well. Pour the egg mixture over the bread; spread and press so bread is covered with the liquid. Cover and refrigerate 30 minutes or longer. Uncover and top with thin slices of tomato and optional roasted bell pepper strips. Sprinkle with the remaining cheese. Bake in preheated 350-degree oven 30-35 minutes. It is done when a knife inserted near center comes out clean. Let stand 10-15 minutes before serving.

PER SERVING: 431 CALORIES (KCAL); 27G TOTAL FAT; (53% CALORIES FROM FAT); 19G PROTEIN; 33G CARBOHYDRATE; 178MG CHOLESTEROL; 530MG SODIUM

Vegetable Frittata

Serves 4

1 tablespoon olive oil
1 cup broccoli, chopped
1 medium carrot, shredded
1 medium onion, chopped
4 large eggs
¼ cup milk
1 tablespoon chopped parsley
salt and pepper to taste
¼ teaspoon Tabasco sauce
1 cup cheddar cheese, shredded
1 tablespoon Romano cheese, grated

Heat oil in 10-inch skillet over medium-high heat. Cook broccoli, carrot and onion in oil about 5 minutes, stirring frequently, until vegetables are crisp-tender. Meanwhile beat eggs, milk, parsley, salt, pepper and Tabasco sauce thoroughly with fork or wire whisk until a uniform yellow color. Pour egg mixture over vegetables and sprinkle with cheese. Cover and reduce heat to low. Continue cooking about 10 minutes or until set in center. Cut into 4 wedges. Serve immediately.

PER SERVING: 184 CALORIES (KCAL); 11G TOTAL FAT; (53% CALORIES FROM FAT); 14G PROTEIN; 7G CARBOHYDRATE; 197MG CHOLESTEROL; 271MG SODIUM. FOOD EXCHANGES: 0 GRAIN (STARCH); 2 LEAN MEAT; 1 VEGETABLE; 0 FRUIT; 1½ FAT; 0 OTHER CARBOHYDRATES

TASTE TESTER COMMENTS:
"I did a double take when I took my first bite of this dish. I was amazed that something so good could also be good for me—and cost effective—all at the same time!"

Spanakopita Quiche

Serves 6

1 package (10 oz.) frozen chopped spinach, thawed, and drained
1 cup cottage cheese
½ cup Feta cheese, crumbled
salt and pepper to taste
⅔ cup buttermilk
3 eggs
2 green onions, minced
1 teaspoon oregano
1 clove garlic, pressed
6 sheets frozen phyllo pastry, thawed
2 tablespoons fine dry breadcrumbs, divided
4 plum or Roma tomatoes, sliced (about ¼" thick)

Coat a 9-inch pie plate with cooking spray; set aside. Press spinach between paper towels until barely moist; set aside. Position knife blade in food processor bowl; add cottage cheese and next 5 ingredients, and process until smooth. Add spinach, green onions, oregano, and garlic; process 45 seconds. Set aside. Working with 1 phyllo sheet at a time, lightly coat each sheet with cooking spray. Fold phyllo sheet in half crosswise to form a 13- x 8-½-inch rectangle, and lightly coat both sides of rectangle with cooking spray. Gently press rectangle into pie plate, allowing ends to extend over edges of pie plate. Repeat procedure with a second sheet of phyllo, placing it across first sheet in a crisscross design; sprinkle 1 tablespoon breadcrumbs over second sheet. Repeat procedure with remaining phyllo and breadcrumbs, continuing in crisscross design, ending with phyllo. Fold in edges of phyllo to fit pie plate and form a rim. Pour spinach mixture into prepared crust; gently arrange tomato slices over filling. Bake at 350 degrees for 55 minutes or until a knife inserted 1 inch from center comes out clean; let stand 10 minutes before serving.

PER SERVING: 193 CALORIES (KCAL); 7G TOTAL FAT; (32% CALORIES FROM FAT); 14G PROTEIN; 19G CARBOHYDRATE; 107MG CHOLESTEROL; 499MG SODIUM. FOOD EXCHANGES: 1 GRAIN(STARCH); 1½ LEAN MEAT; 1 VEGETABLE; 0 FRUIT; 1 FAT; 0 OTHER CARBOHYDRATES

Herb and Spinach Cakes

Serves 6

1 large onion, chopped
3 cloves garlic, minced
1 teaspoon rosemary, crumbled
¼ teaspoon nutmeg
2 packages (10 oz. each) frozen chopped spinach, thawed, drained,
   and squeezed dry
4 medium potatoes, cooked, peeled, and mashed
¾ cup bread crumbs, divided
¼ cup Romano cheese
salt and pepper to taste
2 eggs, separated
1 tablespoon olive oil, divided

Coat a large nonstick skillet with cooking spray, and place over medium-high heat until hot. Add onion and garlic; sauté 5 minutes or until tender. Add rosemary, nutmeg, and spinach; cook 2 minutes. Place spinach mixture in a large bowl; let cool slightly. Add mashed potatoes, ¼ cup breadcrumbs, cheese, salt, pepper, and egg whites; stir well. Divide spinach mixture into 12 equal portions, shaping each into a 3-½-inch cake. Dredge cakes in remaining breadcrumbs. Coat skillet with cooking spray; add 1 teaspoon oil, and place over medium heat until hot. Add 4 cakes, and cook 6 minutes or until lightly browned, turning cakes carefully after 3 minutes. Repeat procedure with remaining olive oil and cakes.

PER SERVING: 210 CALORIES (KCAL); 6G TOTAL FAT; (25%
CALORIES FROM FAT); 10G PROTEIN; 31G CARBOHYDRATE;
67MG CHOLESTEROL; 267MG SODIUM. FOOD EXCHANGES: 1½
GRAIN(STARCH); ½ LEAN MEAT; 1 VEGETABLE; 0 FRUIT; 1 FAT; 0
OTHER CARBOHYDRATES

Pasta Pie

Serves 4

2 tablespoons olive oil
2 small zucchini, sliced
1 tomato, seeded and
  chopped
1 onion, chopped
4 garlic cloves, minced
2 tablespoons black olives,
  chopped
1 teaspoon dried basil,
  crumbled

1 cup cooked Italian sausage,
  crumbled (I substitute a
  good turkey
  sausage)
salt and pepper to taste
4 eggs
1 ½ cups grated Romano
  cheese
6 ounces angel hair pasta,
  cooked
Additional grated Romano
  cheese

Heat 1 tablespoon oil in a skillet over a medium-high heat. Add zucchini, tomato, onions and garlic and sauté until onion is soft, about 3 minutes. Add basil, black olives and crumbled sausage and set aside. Preheat broiler. Beat eggs and 1½ cups cheese in large bowl. Season with salt and pepper. Mix in vegetables and cooked pasta. Heat remaining tablespoon of olive oil in a cast iron skillet (or a skillet that can go under the broiler) over medium heat. Add egg mixture to skillet. Press mixture with back of spatula to even thickness. Cook until frittata is set and golden brown on bottom. Transfer skillet to broiler and cook until the top of the frittata is set, about 2 minutes. Run a knife around the edge of the frittata to loosen. Then take a  large dinner-sized plate and invert the frittata onto it. Cut the frittata into wedges and serve with a little extra Romano cheese on the side.

PER SERVING: 461 CALORIES (KCAL); 28G TOTAL FAT; (55% CALORIES FROM FAT); 23G PROTEIN; 28G CARBOHYDRATE; 184MG CHOLESTEROL; 693MG SODIUM. FOOD EXCHANGES: 1½ GRAIN (STARCH); 2½ LEAN MEAT; 1 VEGETABLE; 0 FRUIT; 4 FAT; 0 OTHER CARBOHYDRATE

Basil Broccoli Tart

Serves 4

1 recipe cream cheese pie crust (see recipe below)
1 teaspoon flour
2 cups fresh broccoli, chopped and steamed or (10 oz. bag) frozen
   broccoli, cooked and chopped
1 cup tomato, chopped (or use canned)
⅔ cup milk
2 eggs
½ cup grated Romano cheese
2 teaspoons dried basil
salt and pepper to taste

CREAM CHEESE PIE CRUST:
1 cup flour
⅛ teaspoon salt
1 (3 oz.) package cream cheese
1 stick butter (unsalted is best)

In a food processor (or do by hand in a bowl with two knives) process flour, salt and cream cheese till it resembles cornmeal. Add butter 2 tablespoons at a time, processing in-between additions (or do by hand, adding butter the same, but using knives to cut into the butter/flour mixture). Turn the dough out and knead slightly, just enough for the pastry to hold together. Preheat oven to 450 degrees. Roll dough to fit a 9-inch pie plate. Press dough into pan. Pierce dough all over with fork. Bake until golden, about 15 minutes. Cool on rack and reduce oven temperature to 375 degrees. Mix milk, eggs, cheese, basil, salt and pepper in a bowl. Arrange broccoli in tart. Pour custard over the top and bake until the tart puffs a bit and lightly browns, about 35 minutes. Cool slightly before cutting into wedges and serving. Spinach salad would be perfect with this wonderful meal!

PER SERVING: 334 CALORIES (KCAL); 20G TOTAL FAT; (52% CALORIES FROM FAT); 13G PROTEIN; 27G CARBOHYDRATE; 114MG CHOLESTEROL; 521MG SODIUM. FOOD EXCHANGES: 1½ GRAIN(STARCH); 1 LEAN MEAT; 1 VEGETABLE; 0 FRUIT; 3½ FAT; 0 OTHER CARBOHYDRATES

Extra Special Eggs Florentine

Serves 6

2 cups mushrooms, sliced
½ cup chicken broth
1 (10 oz.) package ready-cut fresh spinach, stems trimmed
1 onion, chopped
2 tablespoons flour
2 tablespoons milk
1½ cups ham, chopped (or use smoked turkey)
6 eggs
⅓ cup Romano cheese, grated

Melt 1 tablespoon butter in a skillet over medium-high heat. Add spinach and stir until wilted, about 3 minutes. Arrange spinach in bottom of a 13 X 9 baking dish. Melt remaining 2 tablespoons butter in a saucepan over medium-high heat. Add onion and sauté until soft, about 2 minutes, add mushrooms and sauté another 2 minutes. Add flour, stir 1 minute. Add chicken broth and simmer until sauce thickens, whisking constantly, 3 to 5 minutes. Mix in ham. Season to taste with salt and pepper. Preheat oven to 400 degrees. Crack eggs open over spinach, spacing evenly. Spoon turkey mixture around eggs, leaving yolks exposed. Sprinkle Romano over the top. Bake until eggs are just set, about 15 minutes. Serve with muffins or scones.

PER SERVING: 191 CALORIES (KCAL); 10G TOTAL FAT; (47% CALORIES FROM FAT); 16G PROTEIN; 9G CARBOHYDRATE; 213MG CHOLESTEROL; 677MG SODIUM. FOOD EXCHANGES: 0 GRAIN(STARCH); 2 LEAN MEAT; 1 VEGETABLE; 0 FRUIT; 1 FAT; 0 OTHER CARBOHYDRATES

TASTE TESTER COMMENTS:
"Delicious is an understatement!"

Huevos con Tortillas

Serves 6

1 tablespoon olive oil
12 eggs
4 large green onions, sliced
½ red bell pepper, diced
¼ cup cilantro, chopped
2 teaspoons cumin
½ cup jalapeno jack cheese, grated
6 corn tortillas, halved
Salsa (jarred or see page 50 for Saucy Salsa Sauce)

Preheat oven to 425 degrees. Using a non-aerosol oil spray pump, spray tortilla halves with oil and bake for 5 to 10 minutes. Watch them— different brands cook at different rates. Set aside. Beat eggs, the next 5 ingredients and half the cheese in a bowl. Season to taste with salt and pepper. Heat oil in a non-stick skillet over medium heat. Add egg mixture and cook until just set, stirring frequently, about 3 minutes. Divide among plates. Sprinkle remaining cheese over eggs. Stand 2 tortilla halves in each serving. Serve with salsa on the side.

PER SERVING: 255 CALORIES (KCAL); 15G TOTAL FAT; (52% CALORIES FROM FAT); 15G PROTEIN; 15G CARBOHYDRATE; 384MG CHOLESTEROL; 303MG SODIUM. FOOD EXCHANGES: 1 GRAIN(STARCH); 2 LEAN MEAT; 0 VEGETABLE; 0 FRUIT; 1½ FAT; 0 OTHER CARBOHYDRATES

Rise and Shine Breakfast Roll-up

Serves 6

1 whole wheat tortilla
2 large eggs
¼ cup leftover hash browns
⅛ cup jack cheese, grated

Warm tortilla, scramble eggs, warm the hash browns. Fill tortilla with hash browns, scrambled eggs and cheese. Fold and close tortilla. Garnish heavily with salsa, if you're into starting your day with a kick.

PER SERVING: 390 CALORIES (KCAL); 15G TOTAL FAT; (35% CALORIES FROM FAT); 21G PROTEIN; 41G CARBOHYDRATE; 377MG CHOLESTEROL; 541MG SODIUM. FOOD EXCHANGES: 2½ GRAIN(STARCH); 2 LEAN MEAT; 0 VEGETABLE; 0 FRUIT; 2 FAT; 0 OTHER CARBOHYDRATES

Chapter 8
THE EYES HAVE IT—
'TATER COOKERY

W hat I say is that, if a fellow really likes potatoes, he must be a pretty decent sort of fellow." A. A. Milne.

And who could argue with logic like that? The fact is potatoes are an extremely likable vegetable capable of all kinds of culinary creativity.

Solarium tuberosum, more commonly known as potatoes, are members of the nightshade family. Kin to potatoes include tomatoes, eggplant and peppers. Native to the Americas, just like corn, they didn't originate in Ireland, believe it or not.

Easy to grow, great to store and even more wonderful to eat, these terrific tubers offer just about something for everyone—including budget conscientious cooks in need of a few new tightwad recipes to expand their repertoire.

So get out those potato peelers! These spuds are for you—

Potluck Potato Salad

Serves 6

This is the stuff that potluck dreams are made of—real, old fashioned potato salad, the kind your mom used to make.

2½ pounds small potatoes (whatever you have on hand)
3 tablespoons cider vinegar, or to taste
1 tablespoon honey
5 hard-boiled large eggs, peeled and sliced
⅛ cup mayonnaise
2 tablespoons Dijon mustard
1 onion, chopped
1 large celery rib, diced fine
salt and pepper to taste

Cook potatoes in water and drain in a colander. While still warm, peel potatoes and cut into 1/3 inch thick slices. Toss with vinegar and honey  till coated. Then add the rest of the ingredients, seasoning with a generous amount of salt and pepper. Either serve immediately, or cover with plastic wrap and refrigerate for a later use.

PER SERVING: 232 CALORIES (KCAL); 4G TOTAL FAT; (16% CALORIES FROM FAT); 9G PROTEIN; 41G CARBOHYDRATE; 158MG CHOLESTEROL; 152MG SODIUM. FOOD EXCHANGES: 2½ GRAIN(STARCH); ½ LEAN MEAT; ½ VEGETABLE; 0 FRUIT; ½ FAT; ½ OTHER CARBOHYDRATES

TASTE TESTER COMMENTS:
"As the name implies, this is the perfect dish to take to share at a gathering! I received many raves from people who insisted this was the best potato salad they have ever tried. I agree!"
Cost per serving .72

Potatoes Lyonnaise

Serves 6

3 large potatoes, peeled and thinly sliced
2 small onions, thinly sliced
2 tablespoons butter
2 cloves garlic, minced
salt and pepper to taste
⅛ teaspoon paprika

Combine all ingredients in a deep 3-quart casserole dish in layers and press firmly. Cover with casserole cover or seal with foil. Bake in a preheated 375 degree oven till done, about 45 minutes.

PER SERVING: 129 CALORIES (KCAL); 4G TOTAL FAT; (26% CALORIES FROM FAT); 3G PROTEIN; 22G CARBOHYDRATE; 0MG CHOLESTEROL; 229MG SODIUM

Spicy Potato Salad

Serves 6

1 pound small red potatoes
¼ cup olive oil
¼ cup white wine vinegar
2 garlic cloves, pressed
1 teaspoon cumin
¼ teaspoon dried hot red pepper flakes
2 scallions, sliced thin

Boil potatoes in their jackets. When ready, drain and set aside. In a small bowl whisk together the oil, the vinegar, the garlic, the cumin, and the red pepper flakes until the dressing is well combined. Toss potatoes in the dressing, add scallions, salt and pepper to taste. Great with lemon chicken right off the grill.

PER SERVING: 218 CALORIES (KCAL); 14G TOTAL FAT; (55% CALORIES FROM FAT); 3G PROTEIN; 23G
CARBOHYDRATE; 0MG CHOLESTEROL; 9MG SODIUM. FOOD EXCHANGES: 1 ½ GRAIN(STARCH); 0 LEAN
MEAT; 0 VEGETABLE; 0 FRUIT; 2 ½ FAT; 0 OTHER CARBOHYDRATES

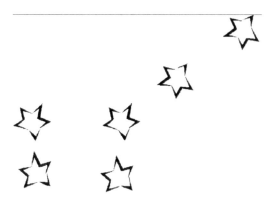

Baked Garlic-y Steak Fries

Serves 6

8 large russet potatoes, peeled
¼ cup olive oil
2 teaspoons garlic powder

Preheat oven to 450 degrees. Cut each potato lengthwise into 8 wedges; toss in bowl with olive oil and garlic powder. Arrange in single layer on 2 baking sheets. Bake until tender and golden, turning potatoes and rotating sheets halfway through baking, about 45 minutes. Serve immediately.

PER SERVING: 162 CALORIES (KCAL); 9G TOTAL FAT; (49% CALORIES FROM FAT); 2G PROTEIN; 19G CARBOHYDRATE; 0MG CHOLESTEROL; 6MG SODIUM. FOOD EXCHANGES: 1 GRAIN(STARCH); 0 LEAN MEAT; 0 VEGETABLE; 0 FRUIT; 2 FAT; 0 OTHER CARBOHYDRATES

TASTE TESTER COMMENTS:

"These are great! I think they will replace my yearnings for the other French Fries that come from the drive through! I used one of those potato-peelers to peel the potato, which left me with a bunch of spiral peels. I baked these for my daughter. She loved her 'curly' fries (slathered with ketchup, of course!")

Cost per serving .38

Double Baked Cheddar Cheese Torpedos

Serves 4

4 large russet baking potatoes, scrubbed and pierced
½ cup milk
2 tablespoons butter
½ cup sour cream (I use low-fat)
1 cup cheddar cheese, grated (I use low-fat)
2 green onions, chopped (partially chop some of the green, too)
1 cup meat (I use leftover anything—taco meat, chicken—whatever)
   or beans
½ cup salsa, for garnish

Preheat oven to 400 degrees. Bake potatoes for an hour or until done. Remove potatoes and let cool 5 minutes before proceeding so you won't end up with third degree burns. Now would be a good time to check your email. Are you back? Okay, let's make torpedoes. Slice your potatoes down the middle horizontally. Scoop out the insides and put into a bowl. You'll want to leave about ¼" of the potato on the skin to make your torpedo sturdy. Spray the torpedoes with a non-aerosol oil spray (see note, page 15) and return them to the oven to get nice and crispy—say 20 minutes or so. While they're cooking, don't go check your email again, make the filling. To do that, all you have to do is smash the remaining ingredients, except the salsa—that is set aside and served on top. But I'm getting ahead of myself. Go back to your bowl of potato innards, add the rest of the ingredients and give it a thorough mixing. Salt and pepper to taste. Your torpedoes should be crisp and nice about now. Fill them up with the potato mixture and return them to the oven for another 10 minutes. Serve them hot with a huge salad and consider it dinner!

PER SERVING: 191 CALORIES (KCAL); 9G TOTAL FAT; (39% CALORIES FROM FAT); 11G PROTEIN; 19G CARBOHYDRATE; 24MG CHOLESTEROL; 401MG SODIUM. FOOD EXCHANGES: 1 GRAIN(STARCH); 1 LEAN MEAT; ½ VEGETABLE; 0 FRUIT; 1 FAT; 0 OTHER CARBOHYDRATES

Mexican Potato Pockets

Serves 4

4 potatoes, cut into ½-inch cubes
½ pound ground beef, cooked and seasoned liberally with garlic
    powder and salt and pepper
1 (15 oz.) can black beans, rinsed and drained (or equivalent
    homemade)
1 cup jarred salsa
1 medium onion, chopped
3 tablespoons chili powder
1 tablespoon cumin
2 teaspoons garlic powder
salt and pepper to taste
¼ cup sour cream
4 sheets (12 inches square) heavy duty aluminum foil

Heat oven to 450 degrees. In a bowl, mix all ingredients except the sour cream. Divide equally among foil sheets (about 1½ cups each), placing mixture on right halves of foil squares. To seal each pocket, fold left side of foil over mixture. Fold in right edge ½ inch; fold again. Fold top and bottom edges the same way, making a little pocket. Place the pockets on a baking sheet and bake for 40 minutes. To open pockets, use scissors and cut a cross in the top of each, then pull back points, being careful when steam is released. Top contents of each pouch with a tablespoon of sour cream.

PER SERVING: 370 CALORIES (KCAL); 12G TOTAL FAT; (28% CALORIES
FROM FAT); 21G PROTEIN; 46G CARBOHYDRATE; 40MG
CHOLESTEROL; 714MG SODIUM. FOOD EXCHANGES: 2½
GRAIN(STARCH); 2 LEAN MEAT; 1 VEGETABLE; 0 FRUIT; 1 FAT; 0
OTHER CARBOHYDRATES

TASTE TESTER COMMENTS:
The perfect dish to satisfy a craving for tasty and
easy Mexican food!"
Cost per serving .98

Potatoes and Trees Soup

Serves 4

1 tablespoon butter
1 small onion, chopped
4 potatoes, cut into ¾-inch cubes
2 cans chicken broth
1 package (10 oz.) frozen chopped broccoli, thawed and drained
1½ cups shredded cheddar cheese
salt and pepper, to taste

In a large saucepan, melt butter over medium heat. Add onion and sauté till soft, about 3 minutes. Add potatoes and chicken broth. Bring to boil, reduce heat, cover and cook for about 15 minutes, or until potatoes are tender. Remove half the potatoes with slotted spoon and set aside. Pour the remaining contents of the saucepan into a blender. Blend until smooth, then return to the saucepan. Mix in reserved potatoes and add the broccoli. Over medium-low heat gradually add cheese, stirring until heated through and cheese is completely melted. Season with salt and pepper and serve. To maximize your carbohydrate download, you could make some Whole Wheat Biscuits. Then again, maybe a salad would be better. No use going into a carb coma for a bowl of soup.

PER SERVING: 243 CALORIES (KCAL); 7G TOTAL FAT; (24% CALORIES FROM FAT); 18G PROTEIN; 29G CARBOHYDRATE; 17MG CHOLESTEROL; 695MG SODIUM. FOOD EXCHANGES: 1½ GRAIN(STARCH); 1½ LEAN MEAT; 1 VEGETABLE; 0 FRUIT; ½ FAT; 0 OTHER CARBOHYDRATES

Mustard Potatoes

Serves 6

4 tablespoons Dijon mustard
2 teaspoons paprika
4 cloves garlic, pressed
2 teaspoons rosemary, crumbled
salt and pepper to taste
12 red potatoes, quartered

Preheat oven to 400 degrees. Lightly grease a roasting pan. In a large bowl, toss together the potatoes and olive oil. Add garlic and spices, mixing well and dump the potatoes into the greased roasting pan. Make sure potatoes are spread out so they'll cook evenly. Bake for about 45 minutes or until the potatoes are fork tender.

PER SERVING: 132 CALORIES (KCAL); 1G TOTAL FAT; (4% CALORIES FROM FAT);
4G PROTEIN; 29G CARBOHYDRATE; 0MG CHOLESTEROL; 135MG SODIUM.
FOOD EXCHANGES: 1½ GRAIN(STARCH); 0 LEAN MEAT; 0 VEGETABLE; 0 FRUIT;
0 FAT; 0 OTHER CARBOHYDRATES

Mashed Potato Crust

2 large potatoes
2 tablespoons butter
salt and pepper to taste
1 small onion, chopped
Oil

Scrub the potatoes well and cut them into chunks. Boil them until soft. Drain and mash. Combine mashed potatoes with butter, salt, pepper, and onion. Mix well. Using a spoon and your hands, press the "potato crust" into a greased 9-inch pie pan. Bake for 20 minutes. Remove from oven and brush the surface lightly with oil. Return to oven and bake another 20 to 30 minutes until lightly browned. Fill with whatever you want. This would be an excellent time to clean out the refrigerator and make something fun. Use your imagination—like leftover veggies, meat, cheese—whatever. It'll make a great pie!

PER SERVING: 73 CALORIES (KCAL); 4G TOTAL FAT; (46% CALORIES FROM FAT); 1G PROTEIN; 9G CARBOHYDRATE; 10MG CHOLESTEROL; 42MG SODIUM. FOOD EXCHANGES: ½ GRAIN(STARCH); 0 LEAN MEAT; ½ VEGETABLE; 0 FRUIT; 1 FAT; 0 OTHER CARBOHYDRATES

TASTE TESTER COMMENTS:
"A fun and versatile recipe! My children enjoyed picking 'the filling'."
Cost per Serving... Varies depending on what is used for filling.
Cost only .20

Spectacular Side Dish Potatoes

Serves 10

5 pounds russet potatoes, peeled and quartered
½ pint sour cream
1 (8oz.) package cream cheese
2 teaspoons garlic powder
1 teaspoon onion powder
2 tablespoons butter
paprika, for garnish

Boil potatoes for 15 to 20 minutes or until potatoes are tender when pierced with a fork. Drain. Mash until smooth. Then, add the next seven ingredients, mashing until thoroughly incorporated. Don't over mash or potatoes will have the consistency of wall paper paste. Place potatoes in a lightly greased 2-qt. casserole and bake at 350 degrees for 30 minutes. Sprinkle with paprika and broil till top is slightly brown.

PER SERVING: 328 CALORIES (KCAL); 15G TOTAL FAT; (40% CALORIES FROM FAT); 7G PROTEIN; 42G CARBOHYDRATE; 41MG CHOLESTEROL; 395MG SODIUM

Classic Potatoes O'Brian

Serves 4

1 small onion, chopped
1 small bell pepper, chopped (you can use red or green)
4 potatoes — cubed
2 tablespoons olive oil
¼ cup beef broth
½ teaspoon Worcestershire sauce
salt and pepper to taste

In a skillet over medium heat, sauté the onion, peppers and potatoes in oil for 4 minutes. Combine broth and Worcestershire sauce and add to pan. Salt and pepper to taste. Cover and cook for 10 minutes or until potatoes are tender, stirring occasionally. Uncover and finish cooking until liquid is absorbed, about 3 minutes.

PER SERVING: 119 CALORIES (KCAL); 5G TOTAL FAT; (34% CALORIES FROM FAT); 3G PROTEIN; 18G CARBOHYDRATE; 0MG CHOLESTEROL; 63MG SODIUM. FOOD EXCHANGES: 1 GRAIN(STARCH); 0 LEAN MEAT; ½ VEGETABLE; 0 FRUIT; 1 FAT; 0 OTHER CARBOHYDRATES

Roasted Rosemary Garlic Mustard Potatoes

Serves 6

4 tablespoons Dijon mustard
2 teaspoons paprika
4 cloves garlic, pressed
2 teaspoons rosemary, crumbled
salt and pepper to taste
12 red potatoes, quartered

Preheat oven to 400 degrees.   Lightly grease a roasting pan.   In a large bowl, toss together the potatoes and olive oil. Add garlic and spices, mixing well and dump the potatoes into the greased roasting pan. Make sure potatoes are spread out so they'll cook better. Bake for about 45 minutes or until the potatoes are fork tender.

PER SERVING: 132 CALORIES (KCAL); 1G TOTAL FAT; (4% CALORIES FROM FAT); 4G PROTEIN; 29G CARBOHYDRATE; 0MG CHOLESTEROL; 135MG SODIUM. FOOD EXCHANGES: 1½ GRAIN(STARCH); 0 LEAN MEAT; 0 VEGETABLE; 0 FRUIT; 0 FAT; 0 OTHER CARBOHYDRATES

Chapter 9
DELIGHTFUL DESSERTS

When my son hugs me, I would swear he's giving me the Heimlich maneuver. I walk away breathless, counting my ribs. It's usually after a good meal that he subjects me to the Death Grip. It's his way of saying, "Thanks Mom" and after my eyeballs stop bulging, I can usually respond with a tussle of his hair.

Men and food: young or old, married or single, no man is unconquerable when there is a kitchen nearby. In fact, I recently read a report saying men actually found the smell of a pumpkin pie baking to be erotic! Give me a break! No wonder great civilizations have fallen. All a woman had to do was put a pie in the oven and poof! Good-bye Rome. Maybe if we all got together and had a global pumpkin pie bake-a-thon, we could disarm the planet and have a shot at world peace. Something to think about, anyway.

There is one other thing about men that is completely predictable and that is the speed with which they consume. Honestly, my husband has eaten a dessert in the time it took to open the fridge and put away the whipped cream. It doesn't get much faster than that. Sometimes I think my husband and the dog have contests to see who can eat faster.

There isn't much that separates a great pie from an ordinary pie. Crust is everything as any seasoned, man-conquering cook will tell you. That and experience. Your pastry has to "look" a certain way before you even consider putting it in a ball and refrigerating it for the roll out. If you handle it too much, you might as well turn it into a doorstop. Pastry is serious business and a great pie demands great pastry.

But desserts are more than mere pies and in my last book, *Healthy Foods*, I gave the recipe for the perfect pie crust. So let's get on with dessert! You'll want to make each one of these desserts more than once-guaranteed.

Banana-Nut Bars

Makes 24 Bars

½ cup honey
1 cup mashed bananas (about 2 very ripe, medium bananas)
⅓ cup oil
2 eggs
1 cup flour
1 teaspoon baking powder
½ teaspoon baking soda
½ teaspoon cinnamon
¼ teaspoon salt
½ cup nuts, chopped
Cream Cheese Frosting — (recipe follows)

CREAM CHEESE FROSTING:
1 (3 oz.) package cream cheese, softened
⅓ cup butter, softened
1 teaspoon vanilla
½ cup honey

Preheat oven to 350 degrees. Lightly grease a 13 x 9 baking dish. Mix honey, bananas, oil and eggs in large bowl with spoon. Stir in flour, baking powder, baking soda, cinnamon and salt. Stir in nuts. Spread batter in pan. Bake 25 to 30 minutes or until toothpick inserted in center comes out clean. Cool completely. Frost with Cream Cheese Frosting. Cut into 6 rows by 4 rows. Store covered in refrigerator.

TO MAKE CREAM CHEESE FROSTING:
Mix softened cream cheese, butter and vanilla in medium bowl. Gradually beat in honey with a spoon until smooth and spread-able.

PER SERVING: 157 CALORIES (KCAL); 9G TOTAL FAT; (49% CALORIES FROM FAT); 2G PROTEIN; 19G CARBOHYDRATE; 26MG CHOLESTEROL; 111MG SODIUM. FOOD EXCHANGES: ½ GRAIN(STARCH); 0 LEAN MEAT; 0 VEGETABLE; 0 FRUIT; 1½ FAT; 1 OTHER CARBOHYDRATES

Pumpkin Cheesecake

Makes 24 Bars

1½ cup graham cracker crumbs
½ cup finely chopped pecans
¼ cup honey
½ cup butter, melted
3 (8 oz.) packages cream cheese, softened
½ cup sour cream
½ cup honey
2 teaspoons cinnamon
½ teaspoon nutmeg
½ teaspoon ginger
¼ teaspoon allspice
1 (16 oz.) can pureed pumpkin
3 eggs

Mix graham cracker crumbs, pecans, ¼ cup honey and butter. Press evenly on bottom and side of a 9 inch un-greased spring form pan. Refrigerate 20 minutes. Heat oven to 300 degrees. Beat cream cheese, sour cream, ½ cup honey and the spices in large bowl on medium speed until smooth. Pour in pureed pumpkin. Beat in eggs on low speed. Pour over crumb mixture. Bake about 1 hour 15 minutes or until center is firm. Cover and refrigerate at least 3 hours before cutting.

PER SERVING: 263 CALORIES (KCAL); 20G TOTAL FAT; (65% CALORIES FROM FAT); 5G PROTEIN; 19G CARBOHYDRATE; 78MG CHOLESTEROL; 197MG SODIUM. FOOD EXCHANGES: ½ GRAIN(STARCH); ½ LEAN MEAT; ½ VEGETABLE; 0 FRUIT; 3½ FAT; ½ OTHER CARBOHYDRATES

Linzer Torte Bars

Serves 20

1 cup flour
½ cup honey
1 cup ground walnuts
½ cup butter, softened
½ teaspoon cinnamon
⅔ cup raspberry preserves, no sugar added—fruit juice sweetened (NO aspartame)

Heat oven to 375 degrees. Mix all ingredients except preserves with spoon until crumbly. Press two thirds of crumbly mixture into un-greased 9-inch square pan. Spread with preserves and finish by sprinkling remaining crumbly mixture on the top, pressing gently into the preserves. Bake 20 to 25 minutes or until light golden brown. Cool completely before cutting. Cut into 8 rows by 6 rows, making a small grid of 48 bars.

PER SERVING: 58 CALORIES (KCAL); 3G TOTAL FAT; (42% CALORIES FROM FAT); 1G PROTEIN; 8G CARBOHYDRATE; 5MG CHOLESTEROL; 22MG SODIUM. FOOD EXCHANGES: 0 GRAIN(STARCH); 0 LEAN MEAT; 0 VEGETABLE; 0 FRUIT; ½ FAT; ½ OTHER CARBOHYDRATES

TASTE TESTER COMMENTS:

"My favorite. I can't believe how easy this was. This was also a very pretty dessert. I must warn you that if you can't wait for it to cool before cutting, be careful you don't burn the roof of your mouth with the hot preserves, I speak from experience. I cut the bars larger than the suggested 48 bars."
Cost per serving .09

Double-Chocolate Bread Pudding

Serves 4

1⅓ cup evaporated skimmed milk
2 tablespoons honey
4 teaspoons unsweetened cocoa
1 teaspoon vanilla extract
4 egg whites, lightly beaten
3½ cups French bread, cubed (½-inch)
1 tablespoon semi-sweet chocolate chips

Preheat oven to 325 degrees. Combine milk, honey, and cocoa in a medium bowl. Stir with a wire whisk until well blended. Add vanilla and egg whites; stir well. Add bread cubes, stirring until moistened. Lightly grease 4 custard cups (6 oz. each). Spoon custard mixture evenly into prepared cups, topping each cup with chocolate chips. Place cups in a 13 X 9 rectangular baking dish and place in oven. Add hot water to dish so that the water comes up almost half way on the cups, but not quite (about an inch or so). Bake for 40 minutes or until a knife inserted in center comes out clean.

PER SERVING: 705 CALORIES (KCAL); 7G TOTAL FAT; (9% CALORIES FROM FAT); 29G PROTEIN; 129G CARBOHYDRATE; 3MG CHOLESTEROL; 1415MG SODIUM. FOOD EXCHANGES: 7 GRAIN(STARCH); ½ LEAN MEAT; 0 VEGETABLE; 0 FRUIT; 1½ FAT; 1 OTHER CARBOHYDRATES

Berry Bread Pudding

Serves 6

4 cups day-old bread, cubed (5 to 7 slices) (or make it really easy, and use old raisin bread)
1 cup berries, your choice (if seasonal, they'll be less expensive than frozen)
½ cup raisins
1½ cups low-fat milk
2 eggs
2 tablespoons honey
1 teaspoon vanilla
½ teaspoon cinnamon
¼ teaspoon nutmeg

Heat oven to 350 degrees. Lightly grease an 8 inch baking dish. Mix all ingredients; let stand 15 minutes. Spread mixture in baking dish. Place the filled dish into a second larger dish on the oven rack. Pour boiling water to a depth of one-inch, into the larger dish or pan. Bake the pudding in its "water bath" for 25 to 30 minutes, or until set and browned.

PER SERVING: 195 CALORIES (KCAL); 3G TOTAL FAT; (15% CALORIES FROM FAT); 7G PROTEIN; 35G CARBOHYDRATE; 65MG CHOLESTEROL; 224MG SODIUM. FOOD EXCHANGES: 1 GRAIN(STARCH); ½ LEAN MEAT; 0 VEGETABLE; 1 FRUIT; ½ FAT; ½ OTHER CARBOHYDRATES

TASTE TESTER COMMENTS:

"Very easy. I used French bread and blueberries. I had fun making this."
Cost per serving .98

Peach Melba

Serves 6

¾ cup honey
1¼ cups water
2 tablespoons lemon juice
6 medium ripe peaches, peeled, halved, and pitted
2 cups fresh raspberries
1¼ teaspoon vanilla extract
12 tablespoons vanilla yogurt, low-fat

Combine ½ cup honey, 1 cup water, and lemon juice in a large skillet; bring to a boil over medium heat. Place peach halves, cut sides down, in skillet; cover and simmer 3 minutes. Turn peaches over, and cook an additional 3 minutes or until tender. Drain peaches; cover and chill. Discard cooking liquid. Position knife blade in food processor bowl; add raspberries and remaining ¼ cup water. Process 1 minute or until smooth. Strain and discard seeds. Combine raspberry puree, remaining ¼ cup honey, and vanilla in a bowl; cover and chill. Serve chilled peaches, drizzled with raspberry sauce.

PER SERVING: 220 CALORIES (KCAL); 1G TOTAL FAT; (2% CALORIES FROM FAT); 3G PROTEIN; 55G CARBOHYDRATE; 1MG CHOLESTEROL; 22MG SODIUM. FOOD EXCHANGES: 0 GRAIN(STARCH); 0 LEAN MEAT; 0 VEGETABLE; 1 FRUIT; 0 FAT; 2½ OTHER CARBOHYDRATES

Fruit-Custard Kuchen

Serves 9

1 cup flour
1 tablespoon honey
¼ teaspoon salt
⅛ teaspoon baking powder
¼ cup butter, softened
1½ cups fresh fruit (or use 8 oz. frozen fruit)
¼ cup honey
1 teaspoon cinnamon
2 egg yolks
1 cup whipping cream

Preheat oven to 400 degrees. Stir together dry ingredients. Work in butter and 1 tablespoon honey until mixture is crumbly. Pat mixture firmly and evenly in bottom and halfway up sides of an un-greased, 8-inch square baking pan. Then arrange fruit in pan. Mix ¼ cup honey with the cinnamon and sprinkle over the fruit. Bake 15 minutes. Blend egg yolks and whipping cream; pour over fruit. Bake 25 to 30 minutes or until custard is set and edges are lightly browned. Serve warm. Refrigerate any remaining dessert.

PER SERVING: 237 CALORIES (KCAL); 16G TOTAL FAT; (60% CALORIES FROM FAT); 3G PROTEIN; 21G CARBOHYDRATE; 97MG CHOLESTEROL; 130MG SODIUM. FOOD EXCHANGES: ½ GRAIN(STARCH); 0 LEAN MEAT; 0 VEGETABLE; 0 FRUIT; 3 FAT; ½ OTHER CARBOHYDRATES

TASTE TESTER COMMENTS:

"This was the winner, even with my son who doesn't eat sweets! I used a berry medley, blueberries, strawberries, blackberries, and raspberries.
I can't wait to try it with apples!"
Cost per serving .28

Applesauce Prune Cake

Serves 16

½ cup butter
½ cup honey
1 egg
1⅔ cups flour
1 teaspoon baking powder
1 teaspoon baking soda
½ teaspoon salt
2 teaspoons cinnamon
¾ teaspoon all spice
1 cup pitted prunes, chopped
½ cup chopped nuts, optional (no one likes nuts at my house)
1 cup applesauce
2 tablespoons powdered sugar (for garnish—totally optional)

Beat butter and honey until mixed and creamy. Beat in egg. Sift dry ingredients together. Add prunes and nuts to dry mixture, then add this mixture to batter. Blend in applesauce. Bake in a greased 9-cup Bundt pan in a 350-degree oven for 1 hour or until it is done. Let cool on rack in pan for 10 minutes before taking it out of the pan. Sprinkle with sifted powdered sugar, if desired.

PER SERVING: 200 CALORIES (KCAL); 9G TOTAL FAT; (37% CALORIES FROM FAT); 3G PROTEIN; 30G CARBOHYDRATE; 27MG CHOLESTEROL; 240MG SODIUM. FOOD EXCHANGES: ½ GRAIN(STARCH); 0 LEAN MEAT; 0 VEGETABLE; ½ FRUIT; 1½ FAT; ½ OTHER CARBOHYDRATES

TASTE TESTER COMMENTS:
"Very delicious, very moist."

Fruit Cobbler
Serves 6

1 cup pancake mix (I like whole wheat)
½ cup regular oats
¼ cup honey
½ teaspoon cinnamon
¼ cup butter, cut into small pieces
6 cups frozen fruit
⅛ cup honey
vanilla low-fat yogurt

Preheat oven to 350 degrees. Combine first 4 ingredients in a bowl; cut in butter with a pastry blender or 2 knives until mixture resembles corn meal. Set aside. Combine your choice of fruit or combination of fruits into a 2-quart casserole, and drizzle ¼ cup of honey evenly over fruit. Crumble oat mixture evenly over the top. Bake for 45 minutes or until cobbler is bubbling. Serve with low-fat vanilla yogurt if desired.

PER SERVING: 264 CALORIES (KCAL); 9G TOTAL FAT; (29% CALORIES FROM FAT); 5G PROTEIN; 43G CARBOHYDRATE; 21MG CHOLESTEROL; 413MG SODIUM. FOOD EXCHANGES: 1½ GRAIN(STARCH); 0 LEAN MEAT; 0 VEGETABLE; 0 FRUIT; 1½ FAT; 1 OTHER CARBOHYDRATES

Very Berry-Lemon Pudding Cake
Serves 6

¼ cup flour
¼ cup honey
⅛ teaspoon salt
⅛ teaspoon nutmeg
¾ cup buttermilk
¾ teaspoon grated lemon rind
¼ cup fresh lemon juice

2 tablespoons butter, melted
2 large egg yolks
2 large egg whites (at room temperature)
⅛ cup honey
1¼ cup berries, your choice or combination thereof

Preheat oven to 350 degrees. Lightly spoon flour into a dry measuring cup; level with a knife. Combine flour, ¼ cup honey, salt, and nutmeg in a large bowl; add buttermilk, lemon rind and juice, butter, and egg yolks, stirring briskly with a whisk until smooth. Beat egg whites at high speed with a mixer until foamy. Add ☐ cup honey, a little bit at a time, beating until stiff peaks form. Gently stir one-fourth of egg white mixture into the buttermilk mixture, then gently fold in remaining egg white mixture. Then add the berries carefully. Pour batter into an 8-inch square baking pan, lightly greased. Place in a larger baking pan; add hot water to larger pan to depth of 1 inch. Bake at 350 degrees for 35 minutes or until cake springs back when touched lightly in center. Serve warm.

PER SERVING: 167 CALORIES (KCAL); 6G TOTAL FAT; (30% CALORIES FROM FAT); 4G PROTEIN; 26G CARBOHYDRATE; 82MG CHOLESTEROL; 138MG SODIUM. FOOD EXCHANGES: ½ GRAIN(STARCH); 0 LEAN MEAT; 0 VEGETABLE; 0 FRUIT; 1 FAT; 1 OTHER CARBOHYDRATES

Chapter 10
MASTERFUL MIXES
SAVE MONEY

O ne of the reasons we're so hooked on mixes is the convenience—you just can't beat how easy they are! But the ingredients of the ready-mixed stuff in the grocery store should have you running the other way. You just don't want to be putting chemicals, artificial colorings and flavorings and various ingredients you can't even pronounce into your body.

In my first book *Healthy Foods*, I gave a wonderful recipe for making a Mega Muffin Mix. Here are a few other mixes that will help you skip the unhealthy and very expensive mixes in the grocery store for these healthy, easy-to-make and even easier-to-use alternatives.

Fabulous Oatmeal Pancake Mix

7 cups unbleached flour or whole wheat pastry flour
2 cups old fashioned oats
8 teaspoons baking powder
4 teaspoons baking soda
2 teaspoons salt

Sift the ingredients together well and store in a sealed freezer zipper bag or plastic container. If you refrigerate, it will last up to six months, otherwise use the mix up in 3 months.

Yield: 9 cups of mix.

Then when you have your mix all done, here is how you make the pancakes:

1 egg, beaten
2 tablespoons melted butter (or oil)
1 cup buttermilk (add a little water if they are still too thick)
1½ cups Fabulous Pancake Mix

To make pancakes, beat the egg and butter (or oil) together with buttermilk and add Fabulous Oatmeal Pancake mix, stirring as you add. Preheat your griddle so a drop of water bounces off when you test (about 375 degrees, if you have an electric griddle), lightly grease the griddle and pour about 1/3 cup of pancake batter on the griddle. When bubbles start to form on top and the pancake loses its shininess, flip it, wait about 20 to 30 seconds and plop it on your hungry breakfast eater's plate.

Mexican Seasoning
an excellent alternative to those expensive envelope seasoning
packets)

2 tablespoons chili powder
2 tablespoons ground cumin
2 tablespoons paprika
1 teaspoon black pepper
1 teaspoon cayenne pepper
1 tablespoon garlic powder
1 teaspoon crushed red peppers (optional)
1 tablespoon dried oregano

Combine all ingredients and place in a sealed container. Makes about ½ cup of seasoning mix.

Italian Seasoning

2 tablespoons dried basil
2 tablespoons dried marjoram
3 tablespoons dried oregano
3 tablespoons dried thyme
2 tablespoons dried rosemary

Combine all ingredients and place in a sealed container. Makes about ¾ cup of seasoning mix.

A Whole Food Speaks

White flour, white rice and white sugar all have different health problems associated with them. You may notice that this book has only one recipe containing sugar—the rest relying on honey, a much better alternative to sugar.

White rice isn't any better. There's nearly no nutrients associated with it, nor is there any fiber. Brown rice is both nutritious and full of fiber. In this book, when a recipe calls for "rice", I write "rice". It's up to you to decide what you want—good, nutritious brown rice or yucky, wallpaper paste white rice (big smile). I'm not biased in any way, am I?

For all my cooking, I use whole wheat flours. For almost everything that means whole wheat pastry flour because it's much finer and perfect for things like cookies, pie crusts, thickening agents, etc. Regular whole wheat flour is best used in heavier things like bread where you don't mind the gluten developing.

You have a choice in this book on which way to go—you can use the White Family of Food: rice, flour and sugar, or try the Whole Family of Food: brown rice, whole wheat flour and honey. Quality nutrition means you need to eat foods as close to their source as possible and that's what whole foods provide.

Chapter 11
OFF TO A GOOD START:
BREAKFAST AND BRUNCH

As the unofficial Queen of Breakfast for Dinner, I thought it only fair to include a substantial amount of recipes for other breakfast aficionados. While breakfast might be the most important meal of the day, it doesn't have to only be enjoyed in the early morning hours. Breakfast is a decent enough meal to be brought out at night even while the rest of the world may be having more substantive fare, like meatloaf and peas.

It is well worth mentioning again that Breakfast for Dinner can not only be a fun treat for the kids, but it can be a definite budget saver, too. All of the breakfast recipes in this section are well under .99 a serving and some might even be under .99 for the entire recipe.

Saturday Morning Pancakes

Serves 8

My 11-year-old daughter Caroline and her best friend Alison made up this recipe one Saturday

1 ½ cups flour
1 ½ cups whole-wheat flour
2 tablespoons honey
2 teaspoons cinnamon
1 ½ teaspoons baking powder

½ teaspoon salt
½ stick butter, melted
1 ½ cups buttermilk
2 eggs beaten

In a large bowl, sift dry ingredients together and set aside. In a smaller bowl, beat together egg, melted butter, buttermilk and honey Make a well in the dry ingredients and gradually add wet ingredients, a bit at a time till incorporated, but don't over mix. Make pancakes as usual on lightly greased hot griddle. Serve hot with maple syrup.

PER SERVING: 265 CALORIES (KCAL); 8G TOTAL FAT; (26% CALORIES FROM FAT); 8G PROTEIN; 42G
CARBOHYDRATE; 64MG CHOLESTEROL; 347MG SODIUM. FOOD EXCHANGES: 2½ GRAIN(STARCH); 0
LEAN MEAT; 0 VEGETABLE; 0 FRUIT; 1½ FAT; ½ OTHER CARBOHYDRATES

Oatmeal Cookie Muffins

Makes A Dozen

1 cup oats
1 cup buttermilk
1 egg
¼ cup honey
⅓ cup butter, melted
1 cup sifted flour
1 teaspoon baking powder
½ teaspoon baking soda
½ cup raisins

Heat oven to 400 degrees. Lightly grease muffin cups or line with paper liners. Combine oats and buttermilk, then add egg and honey. Beat well and stir in butter. Add dry ingredients and mix only until dampened. Fill muffin cups • full and bake for 20 minutes or until done.

PER SERVING: 187 CALORIES (KCAL); 7G TOTAL FAT; (31% CALORIES FROM FAT); 5G PROTEIN; 28G CARBOHYDRATE; 30MG CHOLESTEROL; 173MG SODIUM. FOOD EXCHANGES: 1 GRAIN(STARCH); 0 LEAN MEAT; 0 VEGETABLE; ½ FRUIT; 1 FAT; ½ OTHER CARBOHYDRATES

TASTE TESTER COMMENTS:
"This is the best of the worlds.. a muffin that tastes as good as a cookie!."

Whole Wheat Sweet Scones

Makes A Dozen

2 cups whole wheat pastry flour (available in health food stores)
4 teaspoons baking powder
¼ cup honey
½ teaspoon salt
4 tablespoons butter
2 eggs
1 egg yolk
2 teaspoons vanilla
½ cup sour cream

Heat oven to 450 degrees. Lightly grease a cookie sheet. Sift together flour, salt and baking powder. Cut the cold butter in with a fork or a pastry cutter until well mixed. Do not overwork. Add well-beaten eggs and yolk, honey, and vanilla. Add half the sour cream and then slowly add the rest until it becomes a soft, but pliable dough, mixing only until just blended. Add raisins, if desired. Turn out dough onto a floured board and knead briefly, then roll into a ¾-inch slab. Cut dough into 8 large diamond shapes or triangles. Place on cookie sheet and bake about 15 to 20 minutes.

PER SERVING: 218 CALORIES (KCAL); 8G TOTAL FAT; (32% CALORIES FROM FAT); 6G PROTEIN; 32G CARBOHYDRATE; 90MG CHOLESTEROL; 456MG SODIUM. FOOD EXCHANGES: 1½ GRAIN(STARCH); ½ LEAN MEAT; 0 VEGETABLE; 0 FRUIT; 1½ FAT; ½ OTHER CARBOHYDRATES

Spice 'em Up Hash Browns

Serves 4

2 tablespoons olive oil
1 teaspoon paprika
¾ teaspoon chili powder
¼ teaspoon cayenne pepper
  (or less if you're timid)
salt and pepper to taste
6 ½ cups potato, diced

Preheat oven to 400 degrees. Combine first 6 ingredients in a large bowl; stir well. Add potatoes; stir well to coat. Place potatoes in a single layer on a cookie sheet coated with cooking spray. Bake at 400 degrees for 30 minutes or until browned.

PER SERVING: 171 CALORIES (KCAL); 5G TOTAL FAT; (24% CALORIES FROM FAT); 3G PROTEIN; 30G CARBOHYDRATE; 0MG CHOLESTEROL; 13MG SODIUM. FOOD EXCHANGES: 2 GRAIN(STARCH); 0 LEAN MEAT; 0 VEGETABLE; 0 FRUIT; 1 FAT; 0 OTHER CARBOHYDRATES

TASTE TESTER COMMENTS:

"This was a great way to add some 'zest' to an otherwise ordinary side-dish. I served this with a Mexican omelet and everyone loved it!"

Plum's Puff Baby

Serves 4

My friend and former catering partner Kim Jorgenson has a restaurant called Plums in Costa Mesa, California. Her Puffed Pancake is world renowned and although this recipe isn't it exactly, it's a close second!

4 eggs
1 cup milk
½ lemon, grated rind and juice
½ teaspoon vanilla extract
1 cup flour
½ stick unsalted butter (tastes best, but you can use regular butter)
½ cup powdered sugar
Lemon wedges

Preheat oven to 475 degrees. Whisk together eggs, milk, lemon rind, lemon juice and vanilla Add flour and beat until batter is smooth. Set aside. Place butter in greased baking dish and heat in oven until butter melts. Pour in batter and bake 20 minutes until puffed and golden. Remove from oven and sprinkle with powdered sugar. Serve with lemon wedges and more powdered sugar.

PER SERVING: 368 CALORIES (KCAL); 17G TOTAL FAT; (41% CALORIES FROM FAT); 11G PROTEIN; 43G CARBOHYDRATE; 220MG CHOLESTEROL; 89MG SODIUM. FOOD EXCHANGES: 1½ GRAIN(STARCH); 1 LEAN MEAT; 0 VEGETABLE; 0 FRUIT; 3 FAT; 1 OTHER CARBOHYDRATES

Breakfast Puffs

Makes 15

⅓ cup butter
½ cup sugar
1 egg
1½ cup flour
1½ teaspoons baking powder
½ teaspoons salt

¼ teaspoon nutmeg
½ cup milk
½ cup sugar
1 teaspoon cinnamon
¼ cup butter, melted

Heat oven to 350 degrees. Lightly grease muffin cups. Mix ⅓ cup butter, ½ cup sugar and the egg. Stir in flour, baking powder, salt and nutmeg alternately with milk. Fill muffin cups about two-thirds full. Bake until golden brown, 20 to 25 minutes. Mix ½ cup sugar and the cinnamon. Immediately after baking, roll puffs in melted butter, then in sugar-cinnamon mixture.

PER SERVING: 169 CALORIES (KCAL); 8G TOTAL FAT; (40% CALORIES FROM FAT); 2G PROTEIN; 24G CARBOHYDRATE; 32MG CHOLESTEROL; 201MG SODIUM. FOOD EXCHANGES: ½ GRAIN (STARCH); 0 LEAN MEAT; 0 VEGETABLE; 0 FRUIT; 1½ FAT; 1 OTHER CARBOHYDRATES

Chapter 12
A PLETHORA OF HINTS, TIPS, TRICKS AND OTHER GOODIES

I n my first book, *Healthy Foods*, I included quite a bit of useful information to help families create healthy kitchens and, therefore, healthy meals. In this cookbook I wanted to include some of the most pertinent indexes, references and information so that you would have everything you could ever need to make a healthy recipe–all in one spot! Take a few moments to glance through the nutritional information and tips available in this chapter and then don't forget to refer back to it while you are cooking for your *Frantic Family*!

Recipe _____

SERVES _____

INGREDIENTS:

_____   _____
_____   _____
_____   _____
_____   _____
_____   _____
_____   _____
_____   _____
_____   _____

INSTRUCTIONS:

_____
_____
_____
_____
_____
_____
_____
_____
_____
_____
_____
_____
_____
_____
_____
_____

Recipe _____

SERVES ____

INGREDIENTS:

_____   _____
_____   _____
_____   _____
_____   _____
_____   _____
_____   _____
_____   _____
_____   _____

INSTRUCTIONS:

_____
_____
_____
_____
_____
_____
_____
_____
_____
_____
_____
_____
_____
_____
_____
_____
_____
_____
_____

Recipe _____

SERVES ____

INGREDIENTS:

_____   _____
_____   _____
_____   _____
_____   _____
_____   _____
_____   _____
_____   _____
_____   _____

INSTRUCTIONS:

_____
_____
_____
_____
_____
_____
_____
_____
_____
_____
_____
_____
_____
_____
_____
_____

A Good Cook Cooks

Half the battle to creating a more efficient and healthy kitchen is getting organized and having the ingredients on-hand for healthy choices. In this section I will share with you my "must-have" items. By arming your kitchen with similar ammo, you will be one step closer to healthy, cheaper, quicker meal production.

This tendency toward convenience foods is rather distressing. True, it is helpful to have something to pull out of your hat when you need to fly out the door for baseball practice, but it doesn't have to come in a box from the freezer and go into the microwave. There is a better solution.

Everything in life worth something has taken some effort. This is also true with trying to eat healthier. It will require some effort on your part, but with a little bit of forethought and a few good moves, it won't be too hard. Plus, I would never leave a mom in the lurch without one or two quick tricks—we all need them, don't we?

So let's start in the kitchen. I have a few good tools I wouldn't want to be without. And then I have some real time saving tools which I call my "indentured servants" because these babies make life a little easier.

Here's the list:

Good, sharp knives—a dull knife will make tomato sauce out of your tomatoes. It is a joy to work with a good knife. I have had my Henckle™ chef knife for over 20 years and it's just as wonderful as the first day I bought it. Good knives are a great tool, if they are kept sharpened.

A few cutting boards—working with just one cutting board is a mistake. With all the scary information out there on salmonella and the rest, it might not be a bad idea to be a little more kosher about your cutting boards: use one for vegetables, fruit etc. and one ONLY for meat.

A flat-bottomed wok—another tool I have owned for a long time. This stainless, well-seasoned pan has scrambled eggs and cooked countless stir frys. I truly wouldn't be without it, and the flat-bottom is essential—no fussing with a ring and a wobbly pan on the stove.

Vegetable steamer—Unless you forget about your vegetables in the steamer, you almost can't wreck them. Plus, they're never soggy.

Popsicle molds—cheap and easy dessert for your kids, and you, for that matter. Buy them when you see them and buy a couple of sets. Good luck finding them in the middle of January however.

Stainless or non-aluminum cookware—aluminum has been linked to all kinds of health problems, and rather than debate the issue, why not just get some decent stainless steel pots and pans and forget about it?

Cupcake liners. I don't know why on earth it took me so long to figure out that cupcake liners can be used for muffins, too. I have seen them used that way in bakery muffins, but I guess I'm just a slow learner. Cupcake liners keep clean up to a minimum and really simplify the process.

A stash of Pyrex™ dishes that you can fill and throw in your freezer. If you can get in the habit of doubling your family's dinner, you can stock a mother lode of meals in the freezer with very little extra effort.

A timer. If you are anything like me, your good intentions can turn into burnt offerings. A good working timer with a buzzer you can actually hear is a smart choice.

A quality wire whisk. There is nothing better than a good whisk for beating eggs, making sauces, gravies, etc. An unbeatable have-to-have tool.

Microwave, for quick heat ups, not cooking.

Pizza stone (good bye Pizza parlors!)

Now, bring on the servants! These appliances need to be seen with new eyes.

That isn't just a crock-pot hiding in the dark corners of your cupboard. That's a cook who'll be whipping up something fabulous for you and your family while you're running around all day or at work. Do you see why you need to yank that thing out from the netherworld of your cupboard?

And the bread machine you got as an anniversary present or wedding gift? Your own personal baker! The freezer? A virtual restaurant waiting to be heated up. Your food processor? Your own personal kitchen assistant.

What more could a gal ask for? Every one of these tools gets neglected from time to time, but if you use them, you'll find yourself able to do so much more in the kitchen and it will be so much easier to cook. With a little bit of planning, some good recipes (got 'em right here!) and a willingness to try something new, your kitchen will never be the same.

Pantry Basics

I have said it before, I'll say it again, a well-stocked pantry is a gal's best friend. Not having to duck out to the grocery store just to get dinner on the table is wonderful. Living that way on a day in-day out basis is glorious. I wouldn't exaggerate about such things.

Pantries can either be full of a bunch of stuff you'll never use—like hearts of palm and creamed corn buried in the dark corners or full of things you use constantly. If you're good at stocking your pantry, the only thing you'll need to concern yourself with is rotating your stock (yep, just like a grocery store!)

For newbie pantry stockers, there is an answer and there is hope. Here I come to save the day! It's Healthy Mom to the rescue! I have some basics for you right here in these next few pages. We are talking about healthy stuff here, but understand something also. I am not made out of endless amounts of cash and don't spend frivolously. Even if I were, I wouldn't. So take your time stocking your pantry, look for specials and sales and *then* go crazy buying canned tomatoes.

If you are living in tight quarters and feel you can't afford a pantry, start a massive decluttering plan and start looking. If you're smart and creative, you can always pull a rabbit out of your hat. During the Y2K madness, (okay, I'll admit it!) I had cases of canned goods under my bed, the kids' beds and dressers. I pulled stuff out and rotated with stuff from the cupboards. So it wasn't the most convenient plan, but it worked.

Stocking the Pantry

An important aspect of being able to plan and cook efficiently has to do with what Amy Dacyczyn, the author of The Tightwad Gazette calls The Pantry Principle. The idea behind the Pantry Principle is to stockpile your basics for your pantry so you don't run out. And you do this buying only on sale, with a coupon or at a salvage/scratch and dent-type store. The Pantry Principle liberated me from rigid menu planners, last minute trips to the grocery store, and the best part is that it kept my budget in line.

The Pantry Principle gives you the freedom to plan your meals around what's in your pantry, so that when you do your grocery shopping, you are actually shopping to replenish pantry supplies and not buying a bunch of stuff just for specific meals.

While everyone's pantry might look a little different, here's what's in my pantry and what I would suggest you might want to include in yours; especially if you're going to make any of the recipes in this book! Remember to use the Pantry Principle as you plan your grocery shopping. Never having to run to the store for one or two ingredients because of your "principled pantry" is a gift of time that you give yourself, even more valuable than the money saved.

BAKING SUPPLIES:

Baking powder (Look for one without aluminum sulfate. Try the health
 food store and remember to refrigerate to keep it fresh!)
Baking soda
Sea salt
Cocoa or **carob*** *(I have cocoa—see glossary for explanation)*
Vinegars: rice wine, red wine, balsamic, apple cider
Whole wheat flour*
Whole wheat pastry flour* *(see glossary for explanation on the
 differences in flour)*
Gluten**(helps make bread rise better)*
Kamut flour*
Whole oats*
Buckwheat flour*
Cornmeal *
Whole grain pancake mix*
Sucanat
Unsulphured molasses
Pure vanilla extract

BREADS:

Whole wheat bread
Rye bread
Tortillas: sprouted whole wheat (health food store), corn
Bagels

CANNED GOODS:
Tomato puree
Diced tomatoes
Whole stewed tomatoes
Tomato paste
Pumpkin puree
Pineapple
Apple sauce *(although I make it, I like to have it on hand, too)*
Evaporated milk
Tuna
Green chilies
Beans *(an assortment for emergencies, otherwise I make my own)*

Salsas

Pickles *(an assortment, plus what I've canned—zucchini relish, okra pickles, pickle pickles)*

C O N D I M E N T S:
Soy sauce

Sesame oil

Ketchup

Mustards *(regular yellow, □ijon, honey mustard, coarse)*

Honey *

Jams *(raspberry, wild blackberry, plum and peach that I canned)*

Peanut butter

Almond butter*

Tahini*

S E A S O N I N G S:
Peppercorns *(use a grinder and grind your own. A quantum leap above the already ground stuff)*

Nutmeg nuts *(I bought some at a dollar store and the itty, bitty grater came with it—unbeatable flavor)*

Ground nutmeg *(only get this if you can't find nutmeg nuts and the itty, bitty grater)*

Garlic powder *(NOT salt)*

Tarragon

Rosemary

Bay leaves

Basil

Sage

Thyme

Ginger

Cloves

Mace

Curry powder

Paul Prudhomme's Pasta & Pizza seasoning *(a little pricey, but so good)*

C E R E A L S:
Wheat Chex

Cheerios
Kamut flakes
Whole oats
7 grain cereal
Puffed wheat, millet, kamut, brown rice
Ancient Grains™ Cereals *(President's Choice brand—widely available in supermarkets everywhere)*

PREPACKAGED STUFF:
White macaroni and cheese *(no junky food colorings)*

LEGUMES & GRAINS & PASTA:
Barley *(not pearled)*
Split peas
Lentils
Black beans
Turtle beans
Pintos
White beans
Navy beans
Brown rice *(short and long grain)*
Brown basmati rice
Couscous
Kamut pastas *(we like this better than whole wheat)*

PANTRY VEGGIES:
Potatoes
Onions
Sweet potatoes
Garlic
Assorted winter squashes when in season

REFRIGERATOR:
Milk
Butter
Eggs

Cheeses *(romano, cheddar, jack—block and shredded)*
Tofu
Yogurt *(homemade or store bought)*
Cold-pressed oils *(I have olive oil and safflower)*
Flax seeds
Yeast
Mayonnaise
Worcestershire sauce *(probably not necessary to refrigerate, but I do)*

F R E E Z E R:
Chicken
Beef
Frozen vegetables *(for emergency dinners, otherwise I use fresh and in-season)*
Frozen fruits *(for smoothies)*
Frozen overripe bananas *(ditto)*
Orange juice
Cheeses
Butter
Homemade popsicles

F R U I T B A S K E T:
Apples
Bananas

V E G E T A B L E B I N:
Carrots
Celery

Other than that, whatever I have—either grown or bought from a veggie stand or on sale at the market. I only buy in-season fruits and vegetables, with the exception of apples, onions, bananas and potatoes.
From the bulk bins at the health food store. I keep mine in plastic containers with screw on tops

The Efficient Kitchen
You can have all the latest and greatest tools, "indentured servants" and "principled pantries" in the world and still not have an efficient

kitchen. Efficient kitchens are implemented by doing something with them. They don't just happen on their own.

To make this happen, you need a plan. Not a great big, complicated system that requires tickler cards, menu planning galore and a day off from life to figure it out. Some simple strategies, a few well-thought out rules—and bingo, you have efficiency.

First things first. Dinner. Believe it or not, there are a lot of people out there who don't even think about dinner till around 4:00 or till they are driving home from work. Regardless this is a poor strategy, or really a non-strategy, because the results are always the same: either a late dinner, a microwaved dinner, or fast food.

Awhile back, when I was doing a time management seminar with my friend Demaris Ford, she introduced the Ten O'clock Principle.

The Ten O'clock Principle is simply, that you decide on your dinner for each night by 10:00 AM that morning. However, if you know that Wednesday, for example, is always very busy, then you decide on dinner for Wednesday night on Tuesday night by 10:00 PM. The Ten O' Clock Principle is the same, you just move it around (AM or PM) accordingly. That way, you can prepare! Like take something out of the freezer to thaw, plug something into the indentured servant (i.e. crock-pot) or check to make sure you have charcoal for the barbeque. While this is a great concept for many families, I have simplified it even further for my own family.

Monday—spaghetti or lasagna

Tuesday—Breakfast for Dinner

Wednesday—crock-pot chili (or something crock potty)

Thursday—salad and sandwich supper

Friday—Rubber chicken *(see recipe section, page 33)*

Saturday—chicken burritos or another selection using leftover chicken

Sunday—a chicken stock-based soup

Vegetables and/or plenty of salad is usually served with every meal, except Breakfast for Dinner.

I did this because I basically didn't want to think about it. This schedule still allows me plenty of creativity, and though we don't rigidly follow it, I like the idea of being able to say, "It's Monday, so we're having spaghetti tonight." This summer, we had lots of squash and tomatoes given to us and we grew our own green beans and corn. So we enjoyed the bounty with a vegetable supper and some homemade cornbread or whole grain bread.

Another efficient thing to do is make double or even triple dinner. You can freeze a meal, and put some in the fridge for leftovers. We eat leftover dinner 9 times out of 10 the next day for lunch. –Makes lunch time a snap and I appreciate the time off from having to constantly engage my brain. Sometimes the question about what the next meal is going to be can send me into a downward spiral. Every little bit helps, you know.

REPRINTED FROM HEALTHY FOODS: AN IRREVERENT GUIDE TO
UNDERSTANDING NUTRITION AND FEEDING YOUR FAMILY WELL
(ISBN 1-891400-20-7) www.championpress.com

GLOSSARY OF NEW TERMS

Stumped by an ingredient? With this simple glossary there is no excuse for not making a healthy choice. Use this as a quick reference guide to get acquainted with some new ingredients that can help you convert to a more healthy lifestyle.

Adzuki beans—I don't mention them in this book, but if you run into them, you should know what they are. Similar to black beans, they are small red beans that are the lowest in fat of all beans.

Bok Choy—a big, vegetable thing that looks like a cross between lettuce and cabbage. Great in stir fry.

Brown rice—this is the only kind of rice to buy, although there are tons of different types of brown rice available: short grain, long grain, basmati, for example.

Better Butter—made with half cold pressed oil and half butter, whipped and kept refrigerated in a plastic tub, it's a good option as a spread or when a recipe calls for butter.

Butter—Yes, it is a saturated fat that is lousy for your heart. But in very small quantities (especially better butter), it's okay.

Carob—fake chocolate. What can I say? Sometimes real is better.

Cumin—often used in Mexican cooking, this spice is fabulous in all sorts of roles. You can get it relatively inexpensively at discount stores now.

Expeller-pressed oils—A.K.A. cold pressed. Oils that have been pressed by means of pressure and not chemicals or heat, thereby preserving the essential fatty acids (EFA'S). ALL Cold pressed oils need to be refrigerated after opening, including olive oil. One of the healthiest things you can do is get good, cold pressed oil and keep it refrigerated.

Flax seeds—don't waste your money on flax meal. The essential fatty acids (EFA's) in it won't be worth a nickel. Buy whole seeds, keep refrigerated and grind with a coffee grinder set apart for just this task.

Or I use a little Cuisinart™ that works well for this purpose, too. Use on top of cereal, but don't cook it or good bye EFA's.

Ginger—a strange looking, alien-like root mass that has a positively intoxicating affect on your stir fry. Buy some, freeze it and pull it out to use again and again. *(See Spice Primer, page 167, for using dried ginger.)*

Gluten—gross sounding name, but essential for decent bread. Gluten is what gives bread it's lightness and tenderness. You can buy bread flour (not recommended if it's white flour) or get the gluten. Found at health food stores, mostly.

Greens—if you live in the South, you know what I'm talking about; if you don't then you don't know what you're missing. Mustard greens, turnip greens, kale, collards, creasy greens—all of these will grow with ease in your garden and are delicious and very nutritious. They may be found in ethnic grocers or health food stores. Just don't fix them the way they would in the South, though. Fatback is a no-no big time. Steam well and serve with rice wine vinegar. Yummy!

Jicama—a weird looking root vegetable that sort of looks like a big brown turnip. The good thing about jicama is the crunch factor. It's sweet and good in salads or served with dip.

Kamut—this is an ancient grain, recently rediscovered. Kamut is low in gluten for gluten-intolerant folks and is wonderfully wheat-y for those who can't tolerate wheat, but would love something similar. Full of protein, more so than wheat.

Lentils—are quick cooking and absolutely delicious. It should be a crime to not eat lentil soup in the winter with homemade bread.

Margarine—the ultimate sacrilege in healthy eating. Full of trans-fatty acids, this stuff will age you as fast as going to the beach without sunscreen.

Millet—bird seed. Actually, puffed millet is a great cereal for kids. Also, dried millet is another carbohydrate option instead of rice. Our family goes for the puffed variety. The parakeet is into the dried.

Miso—this is a fermented paste made out of soybeans. Even though it looks like paste wax for your car, it can sure add some body to a weak soup, or make a good soup all by itself with some sliced green onion in it –like at the sushi bar.

Maple syrup—buy the kind that comes from the tree, not the one with a log cabin or a smiling lady on the bottle. It's expensive, but it's real. I get mine at Sam's Club™ where it is a lot cheaper and mix it with a little bit of unsulphured molasses and honey. That stretches it a bit.

Pastry Flour—the whole wheat variety, of course. A gentler, kinder wheat with less gluten than whole wheat, this is an excellent flour for cookies, pies, cakes and muffins.

Quinoa—(keen-wa) yet another ancient grain, highest amount of protein in a grain. Try it instead of rice; make like a pilaf. (There is even a recipe right here in this book for you to try!)

Rice Milk—a milk substitute made from rice. My son drank this by the case as a toddler. Great for milk allergy folks.

Sea salt—much better than commercial salt, there are more trace minerals and less sodium chloride than regular table salt.

Sesame oil—don't forget about this wonderful oil when you're making stir fry. Toasted sesame oil is strong so you only need a little.

Soy Milk—an alternative to cow's milk, this is great for allergic folks, both in cooking and on cereal. Lots of different brands and even flavors. You need to try some to determine which one works for you.

Spelt—another ancient grain that is great for wheat sensitive folks. A nuttier flavor, and slightly heavier, it makes good bread.

Sprouts—There are lots of sprouts out there that are wonderful on salads, sandwiches and cooked in stir fry. I love radish sprouts on sandwiches, my kids beg for a broccoli/mustard sprout blend when we go to the store, and of course, the standard mung bean sprouts are always there. Just be choosy and avoid slimy sprouts like the plague.

Sucanat—stands for Sugar Cane Natural—get it? This is evaporated sugar cane juice. Use like sugar, it's a great healthy substitute.

Tahini—like peanut butter, only made from sesame seeds. Tahini makes a great salad dressing, dip and sauce.

Tofu—some people really get into tofu, but I mainly use silkened tofu in smoothies, or regular tofu blended to substitute for ricotta in a recipe. When my kids were babies, I'd feed them chunks of this. Great toddler food, because they like really bland stuff.

Vinegar—balsamic is wonderful for salads; so is rice wine vinegar. Also try apple cider and red wine vinegars.

Whole wheat—the only type of wheat product you should be buying. If it doesn't say whole wheat, it's not.

On this page you'll find my simple golden rule for healthy, balanced nutrition. I developed this to help simplify the wealth of information that exists on what to eat and what not to eat. You may want to refer to this page before planning your menus, or make a copy and paste it on your fridge. This is a great primer to share with kids, too!

The Golden Rule

Eat whole unprocessed foods and a balance of protein and complex carbs.

Choose your balance of foods from the categories below.

PROTEIN SOURCES:

Eggs, meat and poultry, salmon and tuna, (other fish are fine, too) dairy products, soy products, legumes
(try to eat free-range eggs and poultry, and organically raised meats)

CARBOHYDRATES:

Whole grains, brown rice, vegetables and fruits

FATS:

Cold-pressed mono-unsaturated oils, like safflower oil, properly stored, as well as olive oil and flax oil.
Butter, unsalted and organic if possible, used very sparingly.

BEVERAGES:

Pure, preferably filtered water. Freshly squeezed juice, but not more than a glass a day.

Coffee or tea in very limited amounts—a cup or two a day.

SUBSTITUTIONS, HINTS & STUFF

Every one of the recipes in this book has been tested, tasted and passed by the taste testers (and their families) and by my own family. A lot of the recipes had to be tested, rewritten and tested again, simply because I am the type of cook that measures nothing—not even muffins. I have an idea of proportions, what it should look like and then I just dump stuff into a bowl and more often than not, I'm quite pleased with the result.

I recognize, though, that not everyone is comfortable with such "methodology", so I have provided things like measurements, sizes of pans and oven temperatures. In any case, the whole point of what I'm getting at is, don't be caught up in the running-off-to-the-store-thing if you don't have an ingredient. There are certain things that are essential, obviously, but there are certain things that aren't.

Here's a quick guide for doing things YOUR way, whether or not the recipe says you can or cannot. Recipes are a lot more flexible than we give them credit for, so remember that if you run out of something mid-recipe.

Substitutions:

Buttermilk—use milk and add a couple of teaspoonfuls of vinegar or lemon. I use buttermilk a lot because it gives a dish a lot of complexity and richness without all the fat. Obviously, substitute something non-dairy if milk allergies are an issue. Soy milks and rice milks can easily be used instead of dairy milk. If you'll notice, I don't mention soy cheese or soy yogurt in the book. That's because they taste nasty. Maybe there is one out there that is decent, but thus far my quest for non-dairy cheeses and yogurts has reaped nothing but a gross aftertaste.

Peanut butter or almond butter—either/or works fine—same proportions. For a great sandwich, try almond butter, honey and sliced banana on whole wheat bread...yum.

Chicken broth—can be exchanged for vegetable broth or try the roasted vegetable stock recipe in this book.

Butter—use a little oil instead or skip it entirely. Spectrum Naturals™ has a non-trans fatty acid margarine if you prefer a no-dairy spread. I cannot tell you what it tastes like though.

Sucanat—most of my dessert recipes call for sucanat. (See glossary, page 163, if you don't know what it is) For most recipes, you could probably get away with honey, but use about half as much since it's much sweeter.

Safflower oil—oils are best when they are not cooked. However, adding a little bit of oil to a baked good makes all the difference. Although safflower is the best oil for baking (because of the almost non-flavor), olive oil is healthier.

Beans—you can get them dried or canned. Sometimes I call for canned in a recipe, sometimes I call for dried that you make up yourself. The point is using them how you have them. If you have a ton cooked and in the freezer, please don't run out and buy a can of beans! And don't cook any up if you happen to have a case of Y2K beans in your linen closet. For cooked, just measure out about 1¼ cups per "can" and call it a day.

Mayonnaise—boy, the choices available today—nonfat, low-fat, regular mayonnaise...yikes. Makes a gal dizzy. My suggestion is you use what you like. The full fat stuff isn't exactly great for you, the nonfat stuff is made from weird stuff...a low-fat, premium brand with ingredients you can pronounce is probably the best tactic, although there are other decent mayos from the health food store available.

SPICE PRIMER

• **ANISE**—I never use this, but if you insist on having spices in alphabetical order, you need to start somewhere. Use it in stews, cakes, fish...the list is endless. Whatever turns your key.

• **BAY LEAF**—Used in stews, soup and great with pot roast. Go easy. Bay leaves are strong. I only use ½ a leaf in my stews.

• **BASIL**—Ah, the taste of summer. Who can resist fresh basil and tomatoes from the garden tossed with olive oil and garlic on a plate full of pasta? Dried, it is wonderful in soups, pasta dishes and chicken.

• **CAYENNE**—hot, hot, hot...but good for what ails you. Capsicum, the plant it comes from, is used by herbalists for a whole host of maladies.

• **CHERVIL**—Rhymes with gerbil. Sort of licorice-y tasting with parsley overtones. Why not just use anise and parsley and keep your lazy susan cleared of stuff you'll never use.

• **DILL**—It's not just for pickles. Try some dill sprinkled on fish, chicken or even in a light cream soup.

• **GARLIC**—nectar of the gods, well, bulb of the gods anyway. Garlic has a way of making the most ordinary food gourmet. Try sprinkling garlic powder (not garlic salt) into a prepared box of white cheddar macaroni and cheese. Surprise! It's pretty good. Fresh, though, is best. Squeeze it from a press into almost anything.

• **GINGER**—this is my current flavor of the month. Sprinkle it in your stir-fry, try it on some baked chicken breasts with a little soy sauce and garlic. See the Glossary (page 162) for more info on working with fresh ginger.

• **NUTMEG**—I love nutmeg. If you can find nutmeg nuts and the grater that comes with it, buy it. Once you've had freshly grated nutmeg, the powdered stuff in the jar is beneath you. Obviously an ingredient in baking, it's also good grated on sautéed squash, green beans, and carrots.

• **OREGANO**—A staple in Italian cooking, it's also good in stews and salad dressings.

- **PARSLEY**—every coffee shop in America uses parsley as a garnish. It's also good for indigestion and bad breath.

- **SAGE**—think Thanksgiving. Turkey wouldn't be the same without a liberal sprinkling of sage in the stuffing.

- **ROSEMARY**—spike a roast with garlic and fresh rosemary, and you'll never be the same. Aromatic and wonderful.

- **THYME**—I use this a lot in recipes. It's strong and adds a hint of character to an otherwise pretty standard dish. Use it with chicken, soups and beef.

- **VANILLA**—make sure you get pure vanilla extract, and not vanillin which is fake-o and gross. Pure vanilla adds a whole dimension to just about anything.

This is quite an abbreviated list of spices, but it's a good start. I've skipped a lot of them because they are used so infrequently and just take up room on the lazy susan. Besides, who cares what turmeric is used for anyway? I can't even pronounce it.

Chapter 13
MAKE MINE A MEAL

Sometimes the hardest part about feeding your family good, nutritious food is in the planning itself. As much as I love to cook and plan menus, I really don't enjoy making a detailed grocery list, but I know that's the only way I can achieve my goal of a quick and healthy dinner, as well as getting the family around the table to enjoy it.

Menu-Mailer was born as a result of helping some ladies become more organized in their thinking toward mealtime. I write a column for FlyLady.net weekly and FlyLady (see her site to see what I'm talking about!) challenged the ladies to totally clutter-bust their houses. I provided the menu, recipes and grocery lists and the ladies went bonkers! They loved it and they wanted to do more. Well, to do this on a regular basis was time-extensive and I truly didn't have the time. My husband said people would happily pay for this service and a light bulb went off in my head. Heck, I would pay for this service! And that's how *Menu-Mailer* came to be as popular as it is!

To find out more about Menu-Mailer or to become a regular subscriber, visit Champion Press at www.championpress.com

Note:** on the following pages, two asterisks next to an item denotes an optional item that is used in a side-serving suggestion.

MENU

Day 1: Chicken Stir Fry Supreme
Day 2: Spinach Lasagna
Day 3: Simple Baked Fish
Day 4: RECIPE RAVE: Nacho Stuffed Shells
Day 5: Turkey Caesar Wraps
Day 6: Barbecued Crock-pot Chicken

SHOPPING LIST

MEAT:
2 pounds boneless skinless chicken breasts (buy them by
   the 3# bag, cheaper)
1½ pounds white fish (I use frozen whitefish)
½ pound extra lean ground beef
¾ pound turkey breast (to make 1½ cups cooked chopped
turkey)

CONDIMENTS:
Vegetable oil (I use safflower oil)
1 package (1.25 oz.) low-sodium (if possible) taco seasoning
Tomato ketchup
Worcestershire sauce
Soy sauce
Cider vinegar
Jarred creamy Caesar dressing
Red wine (or substitute broth or water)
Favorite jarred salsa

PRODUCE:
1 bunch carrots (keep on hand)
1 bunch celery
1 3# bag onions (keep on hand)

1 bunch parsley

1 pound asparagus

6 mushrooms

1 head of garlic (have at least one head garlic on hand)

1 lemon

1 avocado

1 head romaine lettuce

1 bunch green onions

1 bunch cilantro

**1 bag baby carrots

**1 or more bunches lettuce for salads

**red potatoes

**1 bunch broccoli

**1 bag fresh washed spinach

**fresh fruit, your choice

CANNED GOODS:

2 cans chicken broth

1 (26 oz.) favorite spaghetti sauce

1 (16 oz.) refried beans (with chilies, if you like)

1 (8 oz.) can tomato sauce (low-sodium, if you like)

1 (2 oz.) can sliced ripe olives

1 (7 oz.) jar roasted red peppers

SPICES:

Oregano

Garlic powder

Ground red pepper

DAIRY/DAIRY CASE:

Butter (keep a pound on hand)

1 dozen eggs (keep a dozen on hand)

1 pound cottage cheese (low-fat, if you like)

1 pound Mozzarella cheese (you need 1½ cups, shredded)

parmesan cheese (you need ½ cup, grated)

low-fat cheddar cheese (you need ¾+ cup grated)

3 12" flour tortillas (try to get whole wheat or substitute

lavish bread, if available)

DRY GOODS:
Flour
1 (8 oz.) package lasagna noodles
1 package jumbo shells (32 to 36 shells)
1 container bread crumbs (you need 1½ cups)
**1 pound brown rice
**1 package egg noodles

FROZEN:
1 (10 oz.) package frozen chopped spinach
**1 small package petite peas

BAKERY:
Your favorite bread to make garlic bread

We always start off the week with a stir fry recipe to get those older veggies used up.

.

CHICKEN STIR FRY SUPREME

Serves 6

1 pound boneless skinless chicken breasts
2 tablespoons butter
2 carrots — diced
1 stalk celery — diced
½ small onion — diced
1 tbsp. chopped parsley
2 tablespoons flour
2 cans chicken broth
1 egg yolk — lightly beaten
¾ cup dry red wine (or water juice or broth)

2¼ teaspoons all-purpose flour
1 pound fresh asparagus spears — cleaned and cooked
1½ cooked carrot — thinly sliced
6 mushrooms — sliced and sautéed
(chopped leftover veggies sautéed, if you have them)

Heat 1 tablespoon butter in medium saucepan; add carrots, celery, onion and parsley. Cook and stir until tender. Stir in 2 tablespoons flour, then chicken broth. Bring to a boil and simmer 30 minutes. Strain; there should be about 2 cups of broth. Stir 1 cup broth mixture into the beaten egg yolk, return to heat for a few seconds. Keep warm. Don't let it get too hot or it'll cook the egg into little scrambled bits-yuck. If that happens, strain the eggs out with a fine wire mesh strainer. Melt remaining butter in large frying pan. Sauté chicken until browned; remove from pan and keep warm. Add remaining chicken broth to pan; mix a little wine (juice or water) with 1½ teaspoons flour and add to pan with remaining wine. Cook and stir until mixture boils and thickens. Return chicken to sauce and heat. To serve, spoon wine sauce over bottom half of 4 plates; spoon egg sauce over top half. Arrange chicken in center of plates. Garnish with asparagus, carrot and mushrooms slices (and any leftover veggies you may have sautéed).

PER SERVING: 233 CALORIES; 12G FAT (49.3% CALORIES FROM FAT); 17G PROTEIN; 11G CARBOHYDRATE; 3G DIETARY FIBER; 73MG CHOLESTEROL; 763MG SODIUM. EXCHANGES: 0 GRAIN (STARCH); 2 LEAN MEAT; 1½ VEGETABLE; 1 FAT.

SERVING SUGGESTION:

Don't forget-this recipe is your own custom version when you add leftover veggies from your crisper. Don't be afraid of the "non measurement" part of this recipe-be creative! A little fancier of a recipe, but still very simple. Serve on egg noodles, if desired and a green salad if your stir fry is lacking in the veggie department.

SPINACH LASAGNA

Serves 6 to 8 (nutrition info for 8)

1 pound cottage cheese
1½ cups Mozzarella cheese — grated
1 egg
1 (10-ounce) package frozen chopped spinach —
  thawed, and well drained
1 teaspoons salt
¾ teaspoon oregano
⅛ teaspoon pepper
1 (26-ounce) jar spaghetti sauce (26 to 32 ounces)
8 ounces lasagna — uncooked
1 cup water

In large bowl, mix cottage cheese, 1 cup Mozzarella cheese, egg, spinach, salt, oregano and pepper. In a greased 9 x 13-inch baking pan, layer ½ cup spaghetti sauce, ⅓ of noodles, and ½ of cheese mixture. Repeat. Top w/ remaining noodles. Sprinkle remaining Mozzarella cheese. Pour water around edges of baking dish. Cover dish tightly with foil. Bake for 1 hour and 15 minutes, or until bubbly, at 350 degrees. Let stand 15 minutes before serving.

PER SERVING: 341 CALORIES; 12G FAT (31.0% CALORIES FROM FAT); 19G PROTEIN; 40G CARBOHYDRATE; 5G DIETARY FIBER; 47MG CHOLESTEROL; 1078MG SODIUM. EXCHANGES: 1½ GRAIN(STARCH); 2 LEAN MEAT; 3 VEGETABLE; 1½ FAT.

SERVING SUGGESTION:

Serve this delicious lasagna with a big, green salad, a bowl of baby carrots and a loaf of garlic bread.

SIMPLE BAKED FISH

Serves 6

1½ pounds whitefish fillets
3 teaspoons melted butter or oil
¼ cup grated Parmesan cheese
¾ cup chopped parsley
1½ cups dried bread crumbs
1½ cloves garlic — minced or pressed
1½ teaspoons lemon zest
salt and pepper to taste

GARNISH:
Lemon wedges
Parsley sprigs

Mix together bread crumbs, parsley, garlic, salt, pepper, Parmesan cheese, and lemon zest. Rinse fillets gently and pat dry. Rub fillets with butter or oil and dip each side in bread crumb mixture. Bake at 325 degrees for 15-20 minutes (uncovered) and check for doneness. Garnish with parsley and lemon wedges.

PER SERVING: 271 CALORIES; 7G FAT (25.3% CALORIES FROM FAT); 29G PROTEIN; 21G CARBOHYDRATE; 1G DIETARY FIBER; 39MG CHOLESTEROL; 449MG SODIUM. EXCHANGES: 1 ½ GRAIN(STARCH); 3 ½ LEAN MEAT; 0 VEGETABLE; 0 FRUIT; 1 FAT.

SERVING SUGGESTIONS:

Serve this easy fish recipe with steamed red potatoes, steamed broccoli and a big green salad.

NACHO STUFFED SHELLS

Serves 6

9   ounces Jumbo Shells (32 to 36 shells) uncooked
½ pound extra-lean ground beef
¾ (1.25-ounce) package low-sodium taco seasoning
    mix
¾ cup water
¾ 16-ounce can refried beans with chilies
¾ cup low-fat cheddar cheese — shredded
½ cup mild, medium, or hot picante sauce
¾ (8-ounce) can low-sodium tomato sauce
¾ (2-ounce) can sliced ripe olives — drained
⅜ cup thinly sliced green onions
OPTIONAL GARNISHES:
Low-fat Cheddar cheese — grated
Avocado
Cilantro — chopped
Salsa

Prepare pasta according to package directions. While pasta is cooking, sauté beef in a large skillet until browned; drain well. Add taco seasoning mix and water; simmer 5 minutes or until thickened. Stir in beans and cheese. Cook until smooth and well-mixed. When pasta is done, drain well. Fill shells with beef mixture (1-2 tablespoons per shell). Combine picante sauce and tomato sauce in a saucepan. Cook until heated, stirring occasionally. Preheat oven to 350 degrees. Spread ½ cup sauce over the bottom of a 9 × 13-inch baking pan that has been coated with cooking spray. Place filled shells side by side on top of sauce; pour remaining sauce evenly over shells. Sprinkle with olives. Cover with aluminum foil; bake 35 to 40 minutes or until thoroughly heated. Sprinkle with green onions. Cover and let stand 5 minutes before serving. Garnish as desired.

PER SERVING : 378 CALORIES; 10G FAT (25.0% CALORIES FROM FAT); 21G PROTEIN; 49G CARBOHYDRATE; 5G DIETARY FIBER; 32MG CHOLESTEROL; 893MG SODIUM.   EXCHANGES: 3 GRAIN(STARCH); 1 1/2 LEAN MEAT; 1/2 VEGETABLE; 0 FRUIT; 1 FAT; 0 OTHER CARBOHYDRATES.

SERVING SUGGESTION:

A big spinach salad would be perfect!

TURKEY CAESAR WRAP

Serves 6

½ cup prepared thick, creamy Caesar dressing
3 (12- inch) flour tortillas or lavish breads
9 leaves romaine lettuce
1½ cups chopped cooked turkey
¾ (7 ounce) jar roasted red peppers — drained
⅜ cup grated Parmesan cheese

Spread a generous 2 to 3 tablespoons Caesar dressing over entire surface of each flour tortilla or lavish bread. Lay 3 romaine leaves on each tortilla, pressing them gently into the dressing. Place turkey and roasted red peppers equally on one half side of each tortilla. Sprinkle Parmesan cheese evenly over the top of everything on tortillas. Roll up each sandwich tightly like a jelly roll starting with the turkey side. Wrap individually and refrigerate for 1 hour. Before serving, cut each wrap in halves, quarters, or 1½ inch bite-size rounds.

PER SERVING: 227 CALORIES; 6G FAT (24.0% CALORIES FROM FAT); 16G PROTEIN; 26G CARBOHYDRATE; 1G DIETARY FIBER; 31MG CHOLESTEROL; 586MG SODIUM. EXCHANGES: 1½ GRAIN(STARCH); 1½ LEAN MEAT; 0 VEGETABLE; ½ FAT; ½ OTHER CARBOHYDRATES.

SERVING SUGGESTION:
Baby carrots and some fresh fruit
would make this easy meal even easier!

BARBECUE CROCKPOT CHICKEN

Serves 6

3 boneless, skinless chicken breasts
1½ cup tomato ketchup
3 tablespoons brown sugar
1 tablespoon Worcestershire sauce
1 tablespoon soy sauce
1 tablespoon cider vinegar
1 teaspoon ground red hot pepper flakes
½ teaspoon garlic powder

Mix all ingredients for the sauce in the crock-pot. Add the chicken, trying to coat it well in the sauce. Cook on HIGH for 3-4 hours, or low for 6 to 8 hours or until chicken is fully cooked all the way through. Then shred or cut up the chicken, and replace it in the BBQ sauce in the pot; mix it all up so all the pieces are coated.

PER SERVING : 266 CALORIES; 3G FAT (10.5% CALORIES FROM FAT); 55G PROTEIN; 1G CARBOHYDRATE; TRACE DIETARY FIBER; 137MG CHOLESTEROL; 369MG SODIUM. EXCHANGES: 0 GRAIN(STARCH); 7½ LEAN MEAT; 0 VEGETABLE; 0 OTHER CARBOHYDRATES.

SERVING SUGGESTION:
Serve with brown rice, steamed baby carrots
and frozen petite peas.

ALPHABETICAL RECIPE INDEX

RECIPE INDEX BY CATEGORY

*a few of the recipes are listed in two categories